te deum

QUESTIONS IN DISPENSATIONALISM

QUESTIONS IN DISPENSATIONALISM

S. Craig MacDonald

Questions In Dispensationalism

ISBN: 978-0-9998394-0-9

Printed in the United States of America

ACKNOWLEDGMENTS

A book may bear the name of the author but it almost always comes to fruition through the combined efforts of a group of people. Questions In Dispensationalism is no exception. It's appropriate here to acknowledge the critical help of this group in getting the manuscript from my head into the form you now hold in your hand.

The completed draft was sent to three trusted colleagues who were asked to review its content. Dr. Mat Loverin, Jim E. Shemaria, and J.M. Shemaria each read the entire manuscript and made comments on what they found helpful, confusing, and in some cases contrary to their own reading of Scripture. Each of these men were gracious and their suggestions led me to make revisions in many places. Had it not been for their suggestions some sections would have been misleading or incomplete.

You should not assume that what you'll read here aligns with their thinking in every instance. In some cases we agree to disagree in the spirit of graciousness that I try to encourage in the last chapter. Proverbs says, "Iron sharpens iron, and one man sharpens another" (27:17). These men sharpened my thinking and my manuscript, often by taking issue with something I wrote. I'm very grateful to them for that perfect balance of candid critique and collegiality that led me to ask them for their help.

After that step in the process I sent the revised manuscript to Sherry Macy and Sharon McGarvey, two trusted friends with serious editing skills. If you ever want to be humbled send something you've written to an eagle-eyed editor who will spot all your errors in grammar, syntax, and punctuation. There wasn't a page that didn't get marked with corrections to bring it into conformity with the rules of writing, and boy, are there a lot of rules!

I quickly realized how important Sherry and Sharon's efforts were to the quality of this book and how tedious I would find that work. I feel a huge debt of gratitude to both of them for offering their expertise even before I had the first draft complete. If you spot a grammatical error of any kind in this book you should assume I missed fixing something they flagged.

TABLE OF CONTENTS

INTRODUCTION

Understanding Your Bible - an Introduction to Dispensationalism (UYB), was first published in 1995, and its reception has been both humbling and gratifying. At that time no follow-up book was planned, but in the years since that time some have expressed an interest in a book that goes a bit deeper into issues within mid-Acts dispensationalism. *Questions In Dispensationalism* (QID) is the response to that interest.

This book assumes you've read UYB and are familiar with the essentials of mid-Acts dispensationalism presented there. QID aims to give you a more thorough understanding of some of the topics from UYB and also discusses some that weren't covered in that book.

Like UYB, this book is written for laypersons, not academics. So you won't find extensive footnotes, a bibliography, or a long list of supportive texts for every point. That's not because there isn't a place for that kind of book, but most people neither want nor need it. QID tries to be simple and straight- forward because, like UYB, it's written for average believers who want to understand their Bible better.

In the years since UYB was first published interest in learning the deeper teachings of Scripture has generally declined. We live in a world that makes convenience and ease a priority, a world in which every truth should have an immediate practical application. Too many churches foster this trend by providing their congregation with nothing but biblical milk (see 1 Pet. 2:2 and Heb. 5:12-13).

By reading QID you're bucking that trend. Its goal is to present more complex biblical content in an easy-to-read format. The average layperson is perfectly capable of grasping biblical meat if it's presented plainly. The benefits of growing in knowledge are well worth the relatively small effort required. So you're to be commended for demonstrating the value you place on learning God's Word.

Each chapter ends with a section titled "Implications and Applications." All theology, including Dispensational theology, has value only to the extent it makes us better disciples. Students of the Word should be "livers" of the Word. After we've studied what the Scriptures say we must ask the question, "So what?" Application is a necessary step so long as it follows knowledge. You're encouraged to interact thoughtfully with this portion of each chapter.

Each "Implications and Applications" section is followed by a short list of questions. These are intended to help you recall the content of the chapter and can be used as a discussion starter if you're using QID in a group setting.

One more thing before we begin. UYB was a linear book, progressively laying out the case for dispensationalism with each chapter building upon those that preceded it. If someone jumps into a middle chapter it doesn't make a lot of sense. QID is structured a little differently. The sections address topics related to mid-Acts dispensationalism; but, while those sections assume you've read UYB, they aren't dependent on one another. As you look at the "Table of Contents" you may find a topic that particularly interests you right now. If so, you shouldn't have any problem going directly to that section and reading it out of order. That said, the chapters within a section often do move with a logical progression and should be read in order.

With that brief introduction let's get to it!

THE TRANSITION
How did we get from there to here, and who came along?

Understanding Your Bible discussed the basics of dispensationalism, focusing on the dispensation of Law and the current dispensation of Grace. Through most of the Old Testament God dealt with the nation of Israel as his special people, giving them unique blessings and privileges (see Ex. 19:5-6; Rom. 9:4-5). As the apostle Paul makes clear throughout his letters, God has set aside the nation of Israel and now deals with Jews and Gentiles without distinction. This change affects a wide range of things from what we eat, how we dress and how we worship to God's plans for our future.

Of all the dispensational changes throughout history none is as interesting or significant as this shift from the dispensation of Law to this current dispensation of Grace. Noah might disagree, but certainly the implications of this change and the amount of relevant biblical content make it worth a very close look.

In this section we'll try to answer several questions:

- When did the change from the dispensation of Law to the dispensation of Grace occur? Can we pin down the point in the biblical narrative when this dispensation began?
- What happened to those Jews who believed Jesus was the Messiah prior to that point? Did they continue as members of the dispensation of Law, did God transfer them into the Body of Christ, or did they become members of both? This question is especially important because some of those believers—namely Peter, James, John, and Jude—wrote letters included in the New Testament, books written after the dispensational change.

Are those books addressed only to believers of the dispensation of Law or are they fully applicable to the Body of Christ?

- How should we understand Paul's practice and teachings on things clearly associated with the dispensation of Law and God's dealings with the nation of Israel? Paul writes at some length, especially in the Corinthian letters, about methodologies God used with the Jews, including miraculous signs. How do we explain a change in dispensations but the continuation of some features characteristic of the previous dispensation?

The fact that we need to discuss these questions indicates the Bible doesn't give an obvious answer to any of them. We can't turn to a specific passage to settle them beyond all disagreement. But that doesn't mean we can't come to some fairly reasonable conclusions by looking at all the relevant verses spread throughout the New Testament and adding together the information they supply. So while there will always be some disagreement, we'll seek to answer these questions with reasonable certainty.

WHEN DID THE DISPENSATIONAL CHANGE HAPPEN?

Trying to pin down the point at which God revealed the mystery of Jew/Gentile equality to Paul may seem like a search for unnecessary detail, but it's worthwhile for at least two reasons. In a general sense, putting together a picture of Paul's conversion and subsequent movements will show us God's great work in extending his grace to everyone without distinction. One could argue that the impact of including the Gentiles without barrier rates second only to the incarnation and its outcomes in terms of God's grace reaching into human history. Answering the question of "when" will also help us when we move to answering the question "who". A firm grasp on the chronology of this part of the biblical narrative turns out to be critical to figuring out what happened to believers from the dispensation of Law who lived across this change.

We'll assume the dispensational change happened at the same time God told Paul that he was setting his special relationship with Israel aside and would deal with Jews and Gentiles without any distinction. It's possible God would begin the dispensation of Grace prior to revealing that secret to Paul, or at some point significantly later, but it's hard to think of a reason he would.

To identify the point of dispensational change we have to combine the four records of Paul's conversion and subsequent movements found in the New Testament, three of which appear in the book of Acts. The first, written by Luke, is his account of Paul's conversion in chapter nine. The second and third are Paul's own retelling of the same events—first to the crowd at his arrest in Jerusalem (Acts 22) and then at his trial before Agrippa (Acts 26). Paul gives a fourth account of his movements during this same period of time in Galatians 1 and 2. Nowhere in any of those passages is there an explicit statement about when Paul received the revelation, but when we look at a timeline of events constructed by combining all four accounts, the most likely point quickly becomes apparent.

We need to start with a map so we can trace Paul's movements before and after his conversion. These events happened in time and space, and we can't get a complete picture unless we understand both.

1. Paul leaves Jerusalem for Damascus to arrest believers
2. His conversion on the road approaching Damascus
3. "Many days" in Damascus
4. About three years in Arabia
5. Return to Damascus
6. Escape to Jerusalem and 15 days with Peter
7. Escape to Caesarea
8. To Tarsus
9. To Antioch to help with that congregation

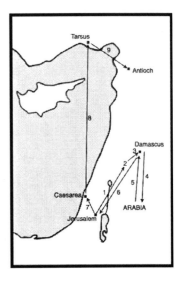

Paul, known by his Hebrew name Saul, was a Pharisee living in Jerusalem working to wipe out those who believed Jesus was the Messiah. His zeal for this cause led him to make a trip to Damascus in search of any there who believed what he considered heresy. As he approached the city he was struck down by a bright light and was told by what was clearly the voice of God that the Jesus he was persecuting was the one speaking to him. Christ told Paul to go into Damascus and await further instructions (Acts 9:1-6).

We get no indication in the Acts narratives that Paul was told by God about the dispensational change during this encounter with Christ on the road into Damascus. In Acts 9:6 and 22:10 Paul is told he'll get further instructions when he gets to Damascus. In the Acts 26 narrative Christ tells Paul that he will be delivered from his own people

16

and from the Gentiles, "...to whom I am sending you to open their eyes...that they may receive forgiveness of sins and a place among those who are sanctified by faith in me" (vv. 17-18). That statement is certainly suggestive of a ministry to Gentiles but doesn't say anything about the setting aside of God's dealings with Israel as his special nation. The Galatians account doesn't mention anything about Paul's conversion experience.

Moving on to the next phase of Paul's movements, Galatians leaves out any discussion of what happened after he got to Damascus. The reason for this omission will eventually become clear. His testimony at trial before Agrippa in Acts 26 also doesn't cover what happened in Damascus.

Luke's record in Acts 9 tells us that after arriving in Damascus Paul remained blind for three days, and for that same period of time didn't eat or drink. Then God directed a believer named Ananias to visit Paul, and though Ananias was at first afraid to do so because of Paul's reputation as a persecutor of believers, he did go to the house where Paul was staying. He was persuaded to do so because God told Ananias that Paul "...is a chosen instrument of mine to carry my name before the Gentiles and kings and the children of Israel" (9:15).

When he arrived at the house, Ananias laid his hands on Paul, his sight was restored, he was filled with the Holy Spirit, and he was baptized (vv. 17-18). Afterward, Paul ate food and "was strengthened" (v. 19). Luke tells us that Paul then spent "some days" with the disciples in Damascus and "immediately he proclaimed Jesus in the synagogues, saying, 'He is the Son of God'" (v. 20).

The narrative in Acts 22 is very similar to Acts 9 and adds that Ananias passed on to Paul what God had told him regarding his future as a witness "to everyone of what you have seen and heard" (v. 15).

At this point, God has not yet given any indications of his big plans for Paul, plans that include a ministry to Gentiles. Nothing has been said to Paul about the setting aside of Israel or the equality of Jews and Gentiles before God. Paul's conversion consists of his new awareness that Jesus was indeed the Messiah, the Promised One of Israel, not the blasphemer he had so violently opposed. Thus, Paul's conversion is no different from that of any other Jew who, after the resurrection, came to believe Jesus was the Messiah. Paul's conversion took place during the dispensation of Law, and though he was told important work was in his future, he had no specifics about the changes on the horizon.

At this point harmonizing the four accounts—the three in Acts and Paul's Galatians record—gets interesting. In the Acts passages we're told Paul went from Damascus back to Jerusalem, but in Galatians Paul provides an additional piece of information not found anywhere in Acts. He writes that he went from Damascus into Arabia and then returned to Damascus.

Before we go further it's important to understand this presents no problem for the truthfulness of any of the accounts. As with the four Gospels, and with Kings and Chronicles in the Old Testament, any biblical record of events is written for the specific readers who would receive it, and for the specific purposes the author had in mind. As we'll see, Paul had a particular goal when he wrote to the Galatian churches that required a very precise and full record of his movements—something that wasn't a factor in the Acts accounts.

After spending some time in Damascus, Paul tells the Galatians he went into Arabia (Gal. 1:7) and then returned to Damascus. Thus, this segment of his movements, his time in Arabia, should be inserted between Acts 9:22 and 23, between Acts 22:16 and 17, and in the middle of Acts 26:20.

How long was Paul in Damascus before leaving for Arabia and how long was he in Arabia? Regarding the first question Acts 9:19 says, "For some days he was with the disciples at Damascus," indicating he was only in the city briefly.

How long was he in Arabia? That's difficult to determine because Paul's only comment in that regard is in Galatians 1:18 where, referring to his return from Arabia to Damascus and from there to Jerusalem he says: "Then after three years I went up to Jerusalem to visit

18

GENESIS

1 WHEN GOD BEGAN creating[a] the heavens and the earth, [2] the earth was at first[b] a shapeless, chaotic mass,[c] with the Spirit of God brooding over the dark vapors.[d]

[3] Then[b] God said, "Let there be light." And light appeared. [4,5] And God was pleased with it, and divided the light from the darkness. So he let it shine for awhile, and then there was darkness again. He called the light "daytime," and the darkness "nighttime." Together they formed the first day.[e]

[6] And God said, "Let the vapors separate[f] to form the sky above and the oceans below." [7,8] So God made the sky, dividing the vapor above from the water below. This all happened on the second day.[g]

[9,10] Then God said, "Let the water beneath the sky be gathered into oceans so that the dry land will emerge." And so it was. Then God named the dry land "earth," and the water "seas." And God was pleased. [11,12] And he said, "Let the earth burst forth with every sort of grass and seed-bearing plant, and fruit trees with seeds inside the fruit, so that these seeds will produce the kinds of plants and fruits they came from." And so it was, and God was pleased. [13] This all occurred on the third day.[h]

[14,15] Then God said, "Let there be bright lights in the sky to give light to the earth and to identify the day and the night; they shall bring about the seasons on the earth, and mark the days and years." And so it was. [16] For God made two huge lights, the sun and moon, to shine down upon the earth—the larger one, the sun, to preside over the day and the smaller one, the moon,

to preside through the night; he also made the stars. [17] And God set them in the sky to light the earth, [18] and to preside over the day and night, and to divide the light from the darkness. And God was pleased. [19] This all happened on the fourth day.[i]

[20] Then God said, "Let the waters teem with fish and other life, and let the skies be filled with birds of every kind." [21,22] So God created great sea creatures, and every sort of fish and every kind of bird. And God looked at them with pleasure, and blessed them all. "Multiply and stock the oceans," he told them, and to the birds he said, "Let your numbers increase. Fill the earth!" [23] That ended the fifth day.[j]

[24] And God said, "Let the earth bring forth every kind of animal—cattle and reptiles and wildlife of every kind." And so it was. [25] God made all sorts of wild animals and cattle and reptiles. And God was pleased with what he had done.

[26] Then God said, "Let us make a man[k] —someone like ourselves,[l] to be the master of all life upon the earth and in the skies and in the seas."

[27] So God made man like his Maker.
Like God did God make man;
Man and maid did he make them.
[28] And God blessed them and told them, "Multiply and fill the earth and subdue it; you are masters of the fish and birds and all the animals. [29] And look! I have given you the seed-bearing plants throughout the earth, and all the fruit trees for your food. [30] And I've given all the grass and plants to the animals and birds for their food." [31] Then God looked over all that he had made, and it was excellent in every way. This ended the sixth day.[m]

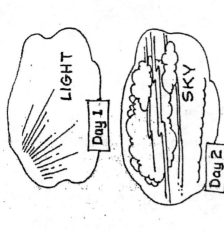

Day 1 — LIGHT

Day 2 — SKY

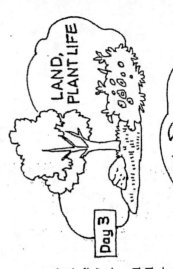

Day 3 — LAND, PLANT LIFE

Day 4

HEBREWS 11

³ By faith—by believing God—we know that the world and the stars—in fact, all things—were made at God's command; and that they were all made from things that can't be seen.ᵃ

ISAIAH 40

²⁵ "With whom will you compare me? Who is my equal?" asks the Holy One.
²⁶ Look up into the heavens! Who created all these stars? As a shepherdᵃ leads his sheep, calling each by its pet name, and counts them to see that none are lost or strayed, so God does with stars and planets!

PSALM 8

8 O LORD OUR God, the majesty and glory of your name fills all the earth and over-flows the heavens. ² You have taught the little children to praise you perfectly. May their example shame and silence your enemies!

³ When I look up into the night skies and see the work of your fingers—the moon and the stars you have made— ⁴ I cannot understand how you can bother with mere puny man, to pay any attention to him! ⁵ And yet you have made him only a little lower than the angels,ᵃ and placed a crown of glory and

JOHN 1

1 BEFORE ANYTHING ELSE existed,ᵃ there was Christ,ᵇ with God. He has alwaysᵃ been alive and is himself God. ³ He created everything there is—nothing exists that he didn't make. ⁴ Eternal life is in him, and this life gives light to all mankind. ⁵ His life is the light that shines through the darkness —and the darkness can never extinguish it.

¹⁰ But although he made the world, the world didn't recognize him when he came. ¹¹,¹² Even in his own land and among his own people, the Jews, he was not accepted. Only a few would welcome and receive him. But to all who received him, he gave the right to become children of God. All they needed to do was to trust him to save them.ᶜ ¹³ All those who believe this are re-born!—not a physical rebirthᵈ resulting from human passion or plan—but from the will of God.

COLOSSIANS 1

¹⁵ Christ is the exact likeness of the un-seen God. He existed before God made any-thing at all,ᵃ and, in fact, ¹⁶ Christ himself is the Creator who made everything in heaven and earth, the things we can see and the things we can't; the spirit world with its kings and kingdoms, its rulers and authori-ties; all were made by Christ for his own use and glory. ¹⁷ He was before all else began and it is his power that holds everything

up of his people—that is, his church—which he began; and he is the Leader of all those who arise from the dead,[b] so that he is first in everything; [19] for God wanted all of himself to be in his Son.

ISAIAH 6

[3] In a great antiphonal chorus they sang, "Holy, holy, holy is the Lord of Hosts; the whole earth is filled with his glory."

ROMANS 8

[19] For all creation is waiting patiently and hopefully for that future day when God will resurrect his children.[b] [20,21] For on that day thorns and thistles, sin, death, and decay[c] —the things that overcame the world against its will at God's command—will all disappear, and the world around us will share in the glorious freedom from sin which God's children enjoy.

[22] For we know that even the things of nature, like animals and plants, suffer in sickness and death as they await this great event.[d] [23] And even we Christians, although we have the Holy Spirit within us as a foretaste of future glory, also groan to be released from pain and suffering. We, too, wait anxiously for that day when God will give us our full rights as his children, including the new bodies he has promised us—bodies that will never be sick again and will never die.

thing you made; everything is put under his authority: [7] all sheep and oxen, and wild animals too, [8] the birds and fish, and all the life in the sea. [9] O Jehovah, our Lord, the majesty and glory of your name fills the earth.

ROMANS 1

[18] But God shows his anger from heaven against all sinful, evil men who push away the truth from them. [19] For the truth about God is known to them instinctively; God has put this knowledge in their hearts. [20] Since earliest times men have seen the earth and sky and all God made, and have known of his existence and great eternal power. So they will have no excuse [when they stand before God at Judgment Day[h]].

[21] Yes, they knew about him all right, but they wouldn't admit it or worship him or even thank him for all his daily care. And after awhile they began to think up silly ideas of what God was like and what he wanted them to do. The result was that their foolish minds became dark and confused. [22] Claiming themselves to be wise without God, they became utter fools instead. [23] And then, instead of worshiping the glorious, ever-living God, they took wood and stone and made idols for themselves, carving them to look like mere birds and animals and snakes and puny[i] men.

Day 5 — MARINE LIFE, BIRDS

Day 6 — ANIMALS, HUMANS

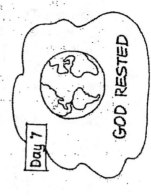

Day 7 — GOD RESTED

GOD'S GOOD CREATION
Genesis 1:1-25

Central Truth: Circumstances in the twentieth century could lead adults to take a pessimistic outlook on their world. Christians, however, can express optimism even in the face of adversity. The Bible clearly teaches that God created the world; and, furthermore, God created a good world.

SUMMARY

1. *God is sovereign.* – Our passage from beginning to end directs our attention to the fact that God is the supreme Lord of the universe. Everything was made by Him and is subject to His power.

2. *We, our world, and all that is in it are subject to God.* – Since God is sovereign, everything else in the universe must be subject to Him. He made the world, and He sustains it. Being subject to His sovereignty, we are all responsible to Him.

3. *Life is uniquely God's gift.* – The Bible's proclamation of faith is that all of life comes as the gift of God. This colors the biblical attitude toward all life and should govern our attitude toward it. This also serves as the basis for the later hope for new life in Christ. The God who gives life out of His grace can renew it through that same grace.

4. *We do not live under the control of the stars or fate.* – You and I are not robots under the impersonal control of the stars. Rather, we and the stars are all under God's control.

5. *God's goodness can be seen in His world through the eyes of faith.* – The world looks different to those who see it from the standpoint of a relationship with Jesus Christ. God is good, and His world is good. In that we can rejoice.

Cephas and remained with him fifteen days." Three years after what? He could mean he went from Damascus to Jerusalem three years after his conversion, or three years after leaving for Arabia, or three years after his return from Arabia to Damascus.

Setting aside for the moment the identification of the beginning point for that three years, it seems likely that his time in Damascus between returning from Arabia and leaving for Jerusalem was relatively short. Acts 9:19-25 tell us that in Damascus Paul preached in the synagogues that Jesus was the Son of God. "When many days had passed, the Jews plotted to kill him" (v. 23), so the disciples helped him make a nighttime escape over the city wall. The other accounts don't give us any information on the time span involved in these various stages except the reference in Galatians to the three years that intervened before his return to Jerusalem.

If we take the earliest point for those three years, Paul's conversion on the way into Damascus, and then subtract a relatively short period of time in that city before and after his time in Arabia, the majority of the three years was spent in Arabia. The obvious question is why Paul spent any time in Arabia. What would he do there? Why would God want him out there for that long? He makes no reference to any ministry in Arabia, any preaching, nor time spent with believers.

In 2 Corinthians 12:7 Paul mentions that he received revelations and uses the plural form. It's reasonable to think the tremendous changes involved in the new dispensation would require some time for God to reveal to Paul and for him to understand and accept them. Think of all the things that are completely different and how difficult those changes would be for Paul.

Nowhere does the Bible tell us when or where God revealed to Paul the secret of this new dispensation. (See Eph. 3:1-3.) If we look for a likely point in the chronology of Paul's movements, his time in Arabia for the better part of three years sure seems a likely spot. So let's continue with this hypothesis and see how the rest of the narrative fits with it.

After returning to Damascus, preaching in the synagogues, and fleeing that city, Paul returned to Jerusalem. It's interesting to think about Paul's thoughts and emotions as he walked back into Jerusalem three years after leaving as a zealous Pharisee on a trip to hunt down the believers, a group of which he now considers himself a member.

Only two of the four narratives give us information about Paul's experiences on his return to Jerusalem. Acts 9:26-30 and Galatians 1:18-19 provide parallel accounts, but at first glance they seem contradictory. Acts tells us the disciples were initially afraid of Paul, but Barnabas took him to the apostles and told them of his conversion and subsequent ministry preaching in Damascus. "So he went in and out among them at Jerusalem, preaching boldly in the name of the Lord" (v. 28). After an unspecified amount of time Paul once again needed the help of the brothers to escape, then went to Tarsus, the city of his birth.

The Galatians record seems to describe a different experience altogether. In 1:18-21 Paul says that upon arriving in Jerusalem he went to visit Cephas (Peter), stayed with him 15 days, and saw none of the other apostles except James, the Lord's brother. After that relatively short stay he says he left for Syria and Cilicia. (Tarsus is the capital of the province of Cilicia.)

In between writing that he stayed with Peter for 15 days and also saw James and writing that he went from Jerusalem to Cilicia, Paul says in verse 20, "In what I am writing to you, before God, I do not lie!" What an odd thing for him to say. It's almost like someone had accused him of falsehood and he's defending himself.

In fact, that's exactly what was going on. In Galatians 1 we see that some in the churches of Galatia had accused Paul of putting himself forward as one proclaiming something new and different. In reality, they claimed, he was just repeating what he'd heard from the apostles in Jerusalem. In verses 11-12 Paul writes, "For I would have you know, brothers, that the gospel that was preached by me is not man's gospel. For I did not receive it from any man, nor was I taught it, but I received it through a revelation of Jesus Christ." Paul then gives this very de-

tailed and precise account of his travels to prove he was not simply repeating the preaching of those men, and, in fact, hadn't even been in
contact with them except for that brief stay with Peter. In Galatians
1:22 he stresses that he was not simply parroting what he'd heard from
the disciples, writing, "And I was still unknown in person to the
churches of Judea that are in Christ. They only were hearing that, 'He
who used to persecute us is now preaching the faith he once tried to
destroy.'"

Paul argues that his message was something new and very different, proclaiming the setting aside of Israel as God's favored nation
and the inclusion of Gentiles as equal in God's sight. His lack of contact
with the apostles in Jerusalem is proof to his accusers that he was not
someone riding the apostles' coattails for personal advancement and
prestige.

What then are we to make of the differences between Luke's
account in Acts 9 of Paul's return to Jerusalem and Paul's record in Galatians 1? Understanding the relationship between the accounts begins
with remembering they were written for different readers and with different objectives in mind. Luke wrote Acts for Theophilus (1:1) to give
him a broad picture of the spread of the gospel outward from Jerusalem
and its Jews to the entire Roman Kingdom and the Gentiles. To do that
Luke records some events, like the Jerusalem Council in Acts 15, in significant detail, while in other places months and even years are covered
in a sentence or two. For example, Acts 18:18 covers the gap between
the second and third missionary journeys in one sentence. The events
and conversations Luke chose to cover in detail are those with particular importance to the dispensational transition that took place during
the 30-year period covered in Acts.

By contrast, in Galatians Paul responded to a very specific accu-
sation that he was nothing more than a traveling preacher seeking fame,
just repeating what he'd heard from the apostles in Jerusalem. For this
reason he goes into detail to show he only had contact with Peter and

James, and only for 15 days. He was personally unknown to the rest of the disciples.

Are there any contradictions between the two accounts? Luke says that, "Barnabas took him and brought him to the apostles and declared to them how on the road he had seen the Lord, who spoke to him" (Acts 9:27). In Galatians we learn that Luke's plural "apostles" refers to Peter and James. Luke writes that Paul preached boldly among the unbelieving Greek-speaking Jews in Jerusalem (9:29), and Paul says he was unknown to the believers except by reputation (Gal. 1:22). Thus, the accounts do not conflict; they only focus on the events from different angles. Luke's is brief because nothing of significance to his purpose for writing the book of Acts happened. In Galatians Paul precisely demonstrates that the accusations being made against him are false.

This collation of the four accounts of Paul's conversion and subsequent movements suggests that God's revelation of the mystery, the change from the dispensation of Law to the dispensation of Grace, took place during the approximately three years Paul spent in Arabia. None of the passages say that specifically. In fact, only one of the four, Paul's account in Galatians, even mentions his time in Arabia, which supports the view that Arabia was the turning point. Again, Paul's purpose in this section of Galatians is to prove the uniqueness of his ministry and its distinction from what the apostles were preaching. If, as he says, his gospel is not something he received from man, but rather received by revelation from God, the obvious questions would be when and where? To answer those questions Paul tells the Galatians about his time in Arabia.

This discussion has assumed Paul received the revelation of the mystery and that the dispensation of Grace began sometime prior to his departure from Jerusalem for Tarsus. Could the revelation of the mystery have happened later? Could it have happened during his time in Tarsus? The answer to that question can most easily be found by moving to the next issue on our agenda for this section, the dispensational position of those who were believers at the time of the dispensational change.

IMPLICATIONS AND APPLICATIONS

Before going on we should pause briefly to think about Paul's conversion and the revelations given to him from a big-picture perspective. What lessons can we learn from his encounters with Jesus Christ and the way they changed the course of his life?

Paul's life parallels Moses' in interesting ways. Both men assumed their lives were on a fixed course until God miraculously spoke to them. When God's time came he grabbed Moses' attention by speaking from a burning bush and Paul's attention with a blinding light on the road into Damascus. Both men received a revelation that led to great beginnings—the nation of Israel and the Body of Christ. They each met with opposition from those who rejected their authority and leadership, and both Moses and Paul remained humble servants the rest of their lives.

Paul fully understood the significance of the revelations given to him and his role as God's instrument in establishing this dispensation (Eph. 3:1-4). He did not hesitate to claim the authority of an apostle (1 Cor. 9:1) and as the one who carried the gospel to the Gentiles (2 Tim. 2:7). Yet, despite all of this, Paul viewed himself first and foremost as a servant of God and his people. In 2 Corinthians 6:3-10 Paul reminds this difficult congregation of what he has endured for their sake and puts it all under the heading of "servant of God" (v. 4).

In a culture so interested in status and standing, Paul's example reminds us we are above all else servants of God, then servants of others. His experience on the road to Damascus transformed not just his theology, but his entire worldview. He was knocked to the ground both literally and figuratively, his ego slain (Phil. 3:4-8), and his focus forever shifted to doing the Lord's bidding.

We can do no better. There's nothing wrong with setting goals and striving to reach them, but our first priority should always be, like Paul's, serving God. This shows up in our our actions and in the way we prioritize our time, energy, and resources. We may be Pauline in our theology, but the apostle to the Gentiles would be at least equally concerned that we follow him as a servant of God and his people in our daily lives.

QUESTIONS

1. Can you reproduce from memory the map earlier in this section, showing the significant geographical points in the narratives of Paul's conversion and what happened at each point?
2. What do you think of the proposed chronology that identifies Paul's stay in Arabia as the time he received the revelations regarding this dispensation?
3. Do you think there's a more likely spot in the chronology? If so, why?
4. What actions in your life indicate you are a servant of God? What are you doing for him? If you were to give yourself a grade, A through F, what letter best reflects your level of servanthood?

WHAT ABOUT THOSE WHO WERE ALREADY BELIEVERS?

To answer this question we will continue looking at the sequence of events in Acts. Any reading of that book shows it to be pivotal, including a clear shift in Luke's focus as he writes. The first eight chapters center on the activities of Peter, events taking place in Jerusalem, and the actions and reactions of the Jews to the preaching that Jesus is their Messiah. Chapters 13-28 focus on Paul, his ministry across the Roman Empire, and the response to his preaching by both Jews and Gentiles. The section in between, chapters 9-12, forms an obvious transition that alternates between the activities of both Peter and Paul, a shift to Antioch, and a congregation in Antioch made up of both Jews and Gentiles.

The significant events of these transition chapters include Luke's account about Peter after his 15-day visit with Paul, who has just recently become a believer (Acts 9:26-28 with Gal. 1:18-20). Imagine the conversations between Paul and Peter for those 15 days! Two men who had been on opposite sides of the most important issue in human history are now brothers in Christ. Eavesdropping on their discussions would have been fascinating and educational.

I think Paul must have quizzed Peter about his time with Jesus, eager to hear stories from the person closest to him throughout his three-year ministry. If, as we've proposed, Paul received the revelation of the mystery during his time in Arabia, he would have enthusiastically told Peter about God's grace now extended to the Gentiles without distinction. How could Paul stay quiet about such a major change in God's dealings with mankind?

Now imagine Peter's reaction to Paul's news. Peter spent three years listening to Christ teach about the coming kingdom, then risked his life to proclaim to the Jews of Jerusalem that Jesus was their Messiah, ready to return and establish that kingdom. Now he's being told all of that has been set aside and Israel is no longer God's special nation.

Peter can be forgiven if he was quietly patient with this new believer's wrongheaded notions.

Luke's account in Acts now shifts abruptly. After having covered Paul's conversion, his time in Damascus, and his return to and escape from Jerusalem in Acts 9, Luke returns in chapter 10 to Peter and his movements. At the end of Acts 9 we read about Peter's healing of Aeneas, a man bedridden for eight years in the city of Lydda, halfway between Jerusalem and the Mediterranean (vv. 32-35). In the next paragraph the believers of the coastal town of Joppa ask Peter to come from Lydda because a beloved disciple named Dorcas had just died. Peter arrives in Joppa and in a beautifully touching narrative Luke describes how Peter raised Dorcas from the dead (vv. 36-42). For reasons not specified, Peter stayed in Joppa "for many days" at the house of Simon, a leather tanner (9:43) and here begins one of the more significant experiences of Peter's life.

Peter had gone up on the flat roof of Simon's house to pray but about noon he got hungry. While he was waiting for food to be brought up he had a vision. In that vision a sheet descended from heaven filled with all kinds of animals, including some that were forbidden to the Jews. A voice said, "Rise Peter; kill and eat" (10:13). Peter, recognizing it as the voice of God refused saying, "I have never eaten anything that is common or unclean" (v. 14). The command was repeated and the second time God added, "What God has made clean, do not call common" (v. 15). Peter was commanded a third time to eat, he still refused, and then the sheet was drawn back up to heaven.

The vision left Peter totally confused, but while he was still puzzling over its meaning three men arrived at Simon's house looking for Peter. Luke has told us who these men are, having described in the previous paragraph the circumstances leading up to their arrival. They were sent by a Gentile named Cornelius, a Roman centurion who lived up the coast in Caesarea. He is described as a "God-fearer," a term used several times in Acts to describe a Gentile who does not become a proselyte but worships the God of Israel and lives a devout life. Luke tells us that those in Cornelius's household were also worshipers of God, even though they were Gentiles.

An angel had appeared to Cornelius and told him that God had taken notice of his open heart, and that he should send for a man named Peter, who was currently in Joppa at the house of a man named Simon, a tanner. Thus we have the three men, two servants and a soldier, arriving at Simon's door asking to speak to Peter.

The next day Peter and some of the disciples from Joppa accompanied these three men for the two-day trip back to Caesarea and Cornelius's house. By the time they arrived Cornelius had called together "many persons" to hear what Peter had to say (v. 27). When he entered the house and saw the group, Peter responded, "You yourselves know how unlawful it is for a Jew to associate with or to visit anyone of another nation, but God has shown me that I should not call any person common or unclean. So when I was sent for, I came without objection. I ask then why you sent for me" (vv. 28-29).

What a fascinating statement! At some point after coming down from Simon's roof Peter figured out the meaning of that vision. He uses the same words God did about the animals in the sheet to describe the Gentiles gathered at Cornelius's house and links what God said in the vision with the group now before him. Neither those animals nor these Gentiles are common or unclean.

In response to Peter's question, "I ask then why you sent for me," Cornelius explained that he did so because of God's instructions, and that those gathered eagerly await whatever Peter has to tell them.

The first words out of Peter's mouth give us another hint of what's going on in this pivotal sequence of events. Peter says, "Truly I understand that God shows no partiality, but in every nation anyone who fears him and does what is right is acceptable to him" (vv. 34-35). The Greek says, "Of a truth I understand," which implies that Peter has now come to understand a reality, a clear fact, namely, that the Gentiles are now equal with the Jews. Peter had correctly said it was unlawful for him to eat those animals in the sheet and to be in the house of a Gentile. The Peter who preached to the crowd at Pentecost would never have said, "God shows no partiality," yet here he declares it as a truth. Why? What has changed?

The answer certainly seems to be his 15 days spent with Paul and the revelation Paul would have shared with Peter. He can be excused for having dismissed Paul's news of the new equality between Jew and Gentile, but after a confirmatory vision from God and now, immediately following that vision, a house full of Gentiles who want to hear his message, Peter says he realizes that equality before God is indeed the truth.

If Peter had any continuing hesitations about this new reality, what happened next certainly resolved them. After telling the household of Cornelius about Christ's death and resurrection and that everyone who believes receives forgiveness of sins, the Holy Spirit "fell on all who heard the word" (v. 44). This amazed the Jewish believers who had traveled with Peter, but it's easy to picture Peter with a smile on his face as he sees before him the evidence of Paul's report and understands the implications of this new truth on the spread of the gospel.

If Peter was pleased to see the gospel open to the Gentiles without distinction, others weren't so thrilled. When Peter got back to Jerusalem some of the disciples confronted him about his actions. Apparently word of Gentiles receiving and responding to the gospel had spread rapidly (Acts 10:1), and Peter came under sharp criticism (v. 2). In response, Peter recounts his vision of the sheet and how the Holy Spirit fell on these Gentile believers just as it had on them. When he saw those at Cornelius's house speak in tongues just like the Jews at Pentecost the reality of their conversion was clear. Peter says, "If then God gave the same gift to them as he gave to us when we believed in the Lord Jesus Christ, who was I that I could stand in God's way?" (v. 17). This silenced the critics and they glorified God for the inclusion of the Gentiles (v. 18).

In the second half of Acts 11 we get another geographical shift, this time to the city of Antioch, 300 miles north of Jerusalem. Luke also gives us a shift in main characters, turning aside from his focus on Peter to talk about others.

One of those is Barnabas, a Jewish disciple who first appeared in chapter 4 among the group who sold personal possessions for the sake of the poor among the Jewish believers in Jerusalem. As noted, he appears again in chapter 9 as the one who intervened and convinced the apostles Peter and James that Paul was indeed now a believer and posed no threat.

Here in chapter 11 we find Barnabas playing a major role with a new group of believers forming in Antioch. Believers from Jerusalem, Jewish men who believed Jesus was the promised Messiah, preached that message in Phoenicia, Cyprus, and Antioch, only to Jews (v. 19). But Luke says there were others who went to Antioch and "spoke to the Hellenists, also preaching the Lord Jesus" (v. 20).

Who are these Hellenists? Specifically, are they Jews or Gentiles? That's a tricky question with significant implications. It's tricky because some manuscripts have the word hellaen, the word for someone who is Greek by nationality, or, by extension, a Gentile. Other manuscripts have hellaenistaes, which only occurs three times in the NT, all in the book of Acts. In the other two occurrences, Acts 6:1 and 9:29, hellaenistaes clearly refers to Greek-speaking Jews, and would almost certainly have the same meaning here. So, were these new believers in Antioch Jews or Gentiles?

The context answers the question of nationality for us. The Greek of v. 19 uses a construction that in English is the equivalent of "on the one hand" and in v. 20 Luke uses the Greek that means "but on the other hand." So a more literal translation would look something like this: "on the one hand some men preached the gospel only to the Jews...but on the other hand some men preached to...." The construction Luke uses requires that the latter recipients of the preaching, those in Antioch, were Gentiles and that the correct reading here is *hellaen*.

This reading fits what Luke says happened next. After hearing that the assembly of believers in Antioch included both Jews and Gentiles, the Jerusalem church sent Barnabas to help the new congregation. Why Barnabas? His name means "son of encouragement" (Acts 4:36), and his intercession on behalf of the newly saved Paul shows him to be a peacemaker who can bridge gaps that will likely develop between the two very different Jewish and Gentile cultures within the same congregation.

Shortly after arriving in Antioch Barnabas went to Tarsus to look for Paul and bring him back to Antioch (11:24-25). This makes sense if the Antioch church was indeed a mix of Jews and Gentiles and if the revelation of equality given to Paul was now accepted by Peter and others as the new reality. Barnabas fetched Paul because he was the ideal person to aid this first congregation containing both Jews and Gentiles.

In Acts 12 the narrative returns once again to Peter, illustrating the transitional nature of this center section of the book. Chapters 1-8 are exclusively about the Jews in Jerusalem, Peter and the other apostles, and the offer of the kingdom to Israel. In chapters 13-28 the focus is on the spread of the gospel to Jews and Gentiles across the Roman Empire through Paul's ministry and the establishment of local churches separate from the synagogues. This section from chapters 9 to 12 forms a transition that alternates between Peter and Paul and the two communities of believers in Jerusalem and Antioch.

In Acts 12 we read of Herod's imprisonment of Peter, Peter's miraculous release, and the death of Herod because of his egotism. Herod's actions and death illustrate another of Luke's themes in this book, namely the response of Jewish leaders to the message of the gospel.

These two incidents with Herod in Acts 12 fall between Luke's mention of Paul and Barnabas taking financial help from the church in Antioch to the believers in Jerusalem (11:27-30) and their return to Antioch (12:25). At this point the center of the action in Luke's book shifts completely from Jerusalem to Antioch. Paul's missionary journeys form the structure of the rest of Acts, and each begins (and two end) in Antioch.

We've just spent considerable time constructing a chronology of this center section of Acts. Why is understanding this sequence of events important? Because now we can answer the question posed at the beginning of this section: what was the dispensational position of those who were already believers before the revelation of the mystery was given to Paul? Did God place them in the Body of Christ or did they remain separate, still within the context of God's special dealings with Israel? The first step in answering this is to identify the point at which Paul received the revelation from God, and we've seen that the most likely place for that is Paul's approximately three years in Arabia. Then we looked at Peter's actions and movements after his contact with Paul to see if these show a shift from what he said and did prior to those 15 days.

Luke's narrative goes almost immediately from Peter's 15 days with Paul, as recorded in Galatians, to his encounter with the Gentiles at Cornelius's house. This seems decisive. By Peter's own words, and as confirmed by the Jews in Jerusalem after his return from Joppa, being in the house of a Gentile and associating with that assembled group violated Jewish standards. Peter explains his decision to do so by referring to his vision of the unclean animals in the sheet. Peter's actions are consistent with Paul's description of Jews in 1 Corinthians 1:22, "For Jews demand signs." Peter heard from Paul about the change God was making, but until it was confirmed to him through miraculous signs–the sheet vision and the Gentiles speaking in tongues—he resisted that truth. After the sheet vision and the Cornelius experience we see Peter and the church in Jerusalem interacting and cooperating fully with the Gentile ministry as led by Paul.

We therefore conclude that those who were believers before the revelation of the mystery to Paul became, by God's sovereign action, members of the Body of Christ with the beginning of the dispensation of Grace. Some of those believers learned of their new position, but it's reasonable to assume many of them did not. This presents no problem and parallels the situation of many believers today who are unaware of truths, like the permanently indwelling Holy Spirit, that are nonetheless a reality in their lives.

This conclusion is supported by what we read in the letters of the New Testament. Paul and Peter each wrote statements that confirm their alignment. For example, in Galatians 2:11-14 Paul recounts a visit by Peter to Antioch that resulted in a confrontation. Everything was going fine until some men arrived from Jerusalem who insisted that Gentile believers were unclean unless they followed the Mosaic law. Peter felt intimidated by these men and withdrew from his association with the Gentile Christians leading other Jewish believers in Antioch to do the same. Paul writes, "I opposed him to his face, because he stood condemned" (v. 11). He then adds, "When I saw that their conduct was not in step with the truth of the gospel I said to Cephas before them all, 'If you, though a Jew, live like a Gentile and not like a Jew, how can you force the Gentiles to live like Jews?'" (v. 14).

This account only makes sense if Peter had accepted the new conditions of the dispensation of Grace and set aside the conditions of the law. Paul's words, "If you, though a Jew, live like a Gentile and not like a Jew..." tells us Peter had made the switch, but the arrival of these legalists from Jerusalem caused Peter to act hypocritically (v. 13). Paul's use of that word indicates Peter was not living according to truth he had accepted.

In 2 Peter 3:15 we read, "And count the patience of our Lord as salvation, just as our beloved brother Paul also wrote to you according to the wisdom given him." If God had two dispensational programs running concurrently we would not expect the leaders of each to be writing instructions to the same believers. Except for the matter of salvation through faith in Christ's substitutionary death, the truths and instructions for the two dispensations would be very different, especially in the area of future events. Peter's endorsement of Paul's teaching ministry to this same group of believers indicates they were in alignment on their instruction.

We also wouldn't expect to find both Peter and Paul relying on the help of Silvanus. The shortened version of his Latin name is Silas, the same man who played a key role in Acts. He accompanied Paul when he left on his first and second missionary journeys and helped Peter when he wrote 2 Peter (5:12). If God was running two dispensations concurrently we would expect these two men to have their own assistants, each within their dispensational context. But instead, Silas is a valued helper to both of them, another indication that Paul and Peter agreed regarding God's dispensational work in the world.

What about Galatians 2:7? In this section, where Paul describes his trip from Antioch to Jerusalem for the purpose of delivering financial aid to those struggling believers (see Acts 11:27-30 for Luke's account of this trip), Paul writes about the reaction of key leaders in that church: "When they saw that I had been entrusted with the gospel to the uncircumcised, just as Peter had been entrusted with the gospel to the circumcised..." (v. 7). Does this mean Paul and Peter preached two different gospels, Paul for the Body of Christ and Peter for the Jews under God's kingdom program?

The answer to the question comes when we understand one of the features of the Greek language. English has a set of prepositions to describe the relationship between two things. Maybe you remember an English teacher using the analogy of a mountain. Anything that describes a position relative to the mountain is a preposition - over, through, to, from, around, etc.

The Greek language has very few prepositions. Instead, for most of those meanings Greek adds a particular ending to the noun (e.g., mountain) that describes the relationship. The addition of this ending puts it in what's called the genitive case. If you look at Galatians 2:7 in the Greek you'll find that both occurrences of the word gospel in verse

7 are genitives. They have that ending. (Note: other endings can be added to form other cases and communicate other meanings.)

The difficulty is that the same genitive case is used for a whole range of prepositions. So the word gospel in verse 7 can mean *gospel of,* or *gospel to.* In the first case, *gospel of,* the content of the gospels is different, and in the latter case, *gospel to,* the content is the same but the targets of the gospel, the recipients, are different. Were Paul and Peter preaching a different gospel or were they preaching the same gospel to different groups?

A decisive argument for one translation or the other of this genitive case cannot be made from this verse. Because the Greek genitive can carry either meaning, we cannot decide from Galatians 2:7 whether God was administering two dispensations and two gospels during this time or if he brought all believers into the Body of Christ. English translations of the Bible may suggest one interpretation or the other, but that's only because those translators chose to use a particular English preposition to translate this use of the word gospel in its genitive case. Galatians 2:7 must be understood in the light of all other passages bearing on the question. While the passages discussed in this section are only a sample, they illustrate the pattern that emerges and indicate this use of the genitive refers to two target groups, not different content.

This is not to say some passages in the epistles of those Jewish leaders, Peter's in particular, aren't difficult to understand in the context of the dispensation of Grace. But if we keep in mind that his readers were Jews raised deep within the context of Judaism with its idioms, customs, and thorough knowledge of the Old Testament, we see nothing that contradicts the truth of the equality of Jews and Gentiles. Peter writes to them using expressions and reference points appropriate to a Jewish readership. In fact, it's noteworthy that Peter uses the word kingdom only once, and he specifically identifies this as "the eternal kingdom of our Lord and Savior Jesus Christ" (1 Peter 1:11) not the millennial kingdom promised to Israel.

On the basis of the information presented in this chapter we conclude that those who were alive and believers prior to the beginning of the dispensation of Grace, including the apostles, became members of the Body of Christ. This means that what are called the General Epistles, or the Jewish Christian Epistles, were written to Jewish members of the Body of Christ and are fully applicable to believers today. The language of those epistles is often very Jewish but that reflects the background of the original readers not their dispensational position.

What then became of the dispensational position of these Jewish believers relative to God's dealings with the nation of Israel? If God placed them in the Body of Christ, did their role in Israel end? This question especially affects Peter and the rest of the apostles because of the promises Christ made to them during his public ministry. For example, he told the Twelve, "Truly, I say to you, in the new world, when the Son of Man will sit on his glorious throne, you who have followed me will also sit on twelve thrones, judging the twelve tribes of Israel" (Matt. 19:28). If the apostles became members of the Body of Christ is this promise overridden?

Since no passage in the New Testament addresses this question, we can't turn to a specific verse and find a clear, definitive answer. The best we can do then is ask what seems reasonable, what is consistent with the way God has acted throughout history. In Romans 11 Paul makes it clear that God has not cast Israel aside permanently and says, "For the gifts and the calling of God are irrevocable" (v. 29). If this is true of God's promises on the national scale it seems clear the same would be true on an individual level. Promises made to the Twelve are equally irrevocable.

How will this play out when that time comes? Will the Twelve participate in the rapture (1 Thess. 4:15) and then return seven years later for the kingdom? That seems like the reasonable scenario. We'll look more closely at the sequence of those events in the chapter on eschatology but at this point it's helpful to remember one of the key principles of Bible study.

Paul tells us that Scripture, when learned and applied, will make the man of God "complete, equipped for every good work" (2 Tim. 3:17). The Bible lacks nothing for God's intended purpose.

We often read passages and wonder about details not supplied. Was Adam present when Eve ate the fruit? Did Noah have to clean up after all those animals while they were on the ark? How will the world respond to the sudden absence of believers after the rapture? The answer to all questions like these is, "It doesn't matter." If the answer was key to what God wanted us to learn he would have supplied it, and the fact we don't have that information tells us it's not important. Being curious about what the Bible says indicates an involved and engaged mind, but ultimately we should focus on the truth God has given us and trust his wise and perfect will for details beyond that.

IMPLICATIONS AND APPLICATIONS

"All Scripture is breathed out by God..." (2 Tim. 3:16), and Paul reminded the Ephesian elders that he "did not shrink from declaring to you the whole counsel of God" (Acts 20:27). It's worth noting that what we call the Old Testament is the only Scripture Paul and the early church had. Paul would reject any theology that ignores or discounts any portion of the Bible. It is true that some portions of Scripture were written to God's people in other dispensations and contain truth fully applicable only to them, but Paul tells us it is all profitable and equips us "for every good work" (2 Tim. 3:17).

On this basis any neglect of the General Epistles is wrong. But understanding that those who were believers prior to the dispensation of Grace became members of the Body of Christ means those books are fully applicable to us and stand equal to Paul's epistles in every regard. Several passages in those books are difficult to understand, but Peter says the same thing about some of what Paul wrote (2 Peter 3:16). The vast majority of what seem like difficult passages in the General Epistles can be understood by keeping in mind their Jewish cultural context.

The authors, with their own Jewish background, wrote using words, phrases, and allusions their Jewish readers would readily understand.

The General Epistles are a rich source of teaching on doctrine and Christian living. James has been called the Proverbs of the New Testament because of the practical wisdom it contains, and 1 Peter teaches us about marriage relationships, church leadership, and suffering for Christ. The apostle Paul, who spent 15 days with Peter after his time in Arabia fellowshipped with him in Antioch and aligned with him at the Jerusalem Council (Acts 15), would be dismayed if he knew some believers effectively discarded the inspired writings of Peter and other brothers who were in Christ before him.

QUESTIONS

1. What chapter of Acts records Paul's conversion? Where would you turn to read about Peter's experience with Cornelius?
2. In what city was the first church to include Gentiles located?
3. Does the Bible translation you normally use indicate the believers in Acts 11:20 were Jews or Gentiles—or is it unclear?
4. How familiar are you with the General Epistles compared to Paul's books? Why?

WHY DID PAUL DO THINGS ASSOCIATED WITH THE DISPENSATION OF LAW?

The dynamics of the changes from one dispensation to the next have varied throughout history. Some, like the change from Innocence to Conscience and from Conscience to Human Government, came about abruptly. Others, like the shift from Human Government to Promise or from Promise to Law, seem harder to pin to a specific time or event. We've already noted that Paul's time in Arabia makes the most likely point at which God revealed the mystery of Jew/Gentile equality, the defining characteristic of the dispensation of Grace, but when and how did this new reality take effect? Peter's experience at the house of Cornelius shows the change had been implemented fully by that point, but even after this event Paul continues to do and write things associated with the dispensation of Law and God's unique relationship with Israel. Why?

Miraculous signs were a key element of God's dealings with Israel as Paul writes in 1 Corinthians 1:22. As noted in Understanding Your Bible, indirect miracles first appeared when God began working exclusively with Israel, and we would expect them to disappear when that relationship was set aside. Yet in Acts we read about Paul healing a lame man (14:8-10), casting out a demon (16:18), and doing "extraordinary miracles" (19:11). Describing his time with the church in Corinth he writes, "The signs of a true apostle were performed among you with utmost patience, with signs and wonders and mighty works" (2 Cor. 12:12). In 1 Corinthians Paul writes to them about the correct practice of the sign gifts, including miracles, tongues, and prophecy (see 1 Cor. 12:8-10 and chapter 14). How do we explain this apparent contradiction between a dispensational change and some of Paul's actions and teachings that best fit the previous dispensation?

For more than 1,400 years Israel held a position as God's special people. In Exodus 19:5-6 we read, "Now therefore, if you will indeed obey my voice and keep my covenant, you shall be my treasured possession among all peoples, for all the earth is mine; and you shall be to me a kingdom of priests and a holy nation." Though his unique relationship with that nation is currently suspended, we know he will once again elevate Israel to that status, "For the gifts and the calling of God are irrevocable" (Rom. 11:29).

During this intervening dispensation of Grace we must distinguish between the nation of Israel and individual Jews. While God has set aside his special relationship with the nation of Israel, his love for individual Jews remains constant. This distinction helps us understand Paul's words in Romans 9:1-5 where he writes that, "I could wish that I myself were accursed and cut off from Christ for the sake of my brothers, my kinsmen according to the flesh" (v. 3). God's love and grace are never withdrawn from anyone, including Jews, because he is patient, "not wishing that any should perish, but that all should reach repentance" (2 Peter 3:9). To this end God used a time of transition so that Jewish individuals could clearly see the results of the nation's hardened hearts and repent. Precisely because of that hardness, and because "Jews demand signs" (1 Cor. 1:22), Paul did miraculous signs early in his ministry so his message of Jew/Gentile equality would be accredited before them (2 Cor. 2:12). Just as many Jews accepted Jesus' claims to be the Messiah after they saw the miraculous signs he did (John 2:23), Paul's miracles authenticated his message of equality. That's why he says the signs that accredit a true apostle were done among the Corinthians.

It's helpful to note the background of Paul's letters in which he discusses the practice of sign gifts associated with God's program for Israel, and the circumstances surrounding Paul's use of them in Acts. Among the epistles, only the two letters to the church in Corinth discuss the practice of the miraculous gifts. When we look in Acts 18 at how the Corinthian church got started, we see an interesting series of events that help us understand this.

40

The text of Acts 18:2 suggests the Jews Aquila and Priscilla, recently arrived in Corinth from Rome, were already believers by the time Paul met them there. As was his habit, Paul went first to the synagogue in Corinth (v. 4). When opposition from the Jews increased Paul left and began meeting with the small group of Jewish converts at the house of Titius Justus, a "worshiper of God," a term used in Acts that indicates he was a Gentile who worshiped at the synagogue, similar to Cornelius in Acts 10. The text tells us Titius Justus lived next door to the synagogue and that one of the early converts attending this new church was Crispus who had been the president of the synagogue. His replacement as president was Sosthenes who we read in 1 Corinthians 1:1 also became a believer. All of these details tell us the Corinthian congregation had a particularly Jewish makeup, and its location right next to the synagogue put it in a strongly Jewish environment. These details help us understand why Paul wrote to this particular church about the practice of sign gifts.

The Corinthian setting illustrates that during a short transition period God continued a methodology suited to the Jewish people who he says require miraculous signs. This was done so they would see and believe that Paul's message regarding Christ and equality was indeed of divine origin and that Gentile converts were accepted and empowered by God. Paul's miracles in other cities and miracles done by Gentiles serve this same purpose—accrediting Paul's message before Israel in the hope that at least some individual Jews would repent.

Just as Israel rejected Christ despite the miracles he performed, so the majority eventually rejected Paul and his message. They would not accept that Jesus was the Messiah who died for their sins or that Gentiles were now on equal footing with them. So after this transitional period the practice of miraculous signs was withdrawn. This explains why no mention is made of sign miracles in any of Paul's letters written after his third missionary journey. The progression of this transition can also be seen in Paul's declaration three times in three different locations, moving from east to west, that because of Israel's hardness he is turning to the Gentiles (Acts 13:46; 18:6; 28:28). The transitional use of a Jewish methodology helps us understand a couple of additional things that might otherwise seem confusing. As discussed in *Understanding Your Bible,* water baptism was always a Jewish purification ritual used in a variety of situations including the ordination of priests and as the final step in a Gentile proselyte's process of becoming a full member of Israel. Why then did Paul practice water baptism?

The only place in Paul's letters in which water baptism is discussed is 1 Corinthians, the same church in which sign gifts are practiced, a congregation with a uniquely Jewish context. (Note: it is correctly agreed by many critical commentaries that Rom. 6:3-4, Gal. 3:27, and Eph. 4:5 refer to Christ's baptism of death as he said in Mark 10:38-39 and Luke 12:50.) Paul also stresses that he baptized very few and was not sent to baptize (1 Cor. 1:14-17; cf. Matt. 28:19). In Acts the only mention of Paul baptizing converts is in Philippi, where he baptized Lydia, like Titius Justus and Cornelius, another "worshiper of God" (Acts 16:14), and the Philippian jailor and his household, perhaps so they would be accepted by the fledgling group of Jewish believers in that city. The Jewish ritual of water baptism played a very minor role in Paul's ministry, appeared only early in his ministry and was minimized in his own assessment of his divine calling.

Consistent with this limited transitional use of a Jewish methodology is Paul's statement in 1 Corinthians 13:8-10 that tongues would pass away. Since this passage is so critical to understanding the dynamics of the transition period, it warrants a closer look. The effort required to understand Paul's use of very specific Greek words will pay off in a clear picture of the transitional nature of some spiritual gifts.

The very words of Scripture were directed by God, so in any passage those words are important. Some English versions do better than others at accurately translating the Greek, and in the case of 1 Corinthians 13:8-10 the New American Standard Bible is among those that do a good job.

> Love never fails;
> but if there are gifts of prophecy, they will be done
> away;
> if there are tongues, they will cease;
> if there is knowledge, it will be done away.
> For we know in part and we prophesy in part; but
> when the perfect comes, the partial will be done away.

Several key features should be noted. The first is that, as is evident in this NASB translation, the Greek verb *katargeo*, here translated, "will be done away," is used by Paul to describe the cessation of both prophecy and knowledge. It's difficult to understand why some versions use a different English word in these two phrases where the Greek is identical.

A different verb, *pauo*, describes the end of tongues ("they will cease").

> Love never fails;
> but if there are gifts of prophecy, they will be done away
> (*katargeo*);
> if there are tongues, they will cease (*pauo*);
> if there is knowledge, it will be done away (*katargeo*).
> For we know in part and we prophesy in part; but when the
> perfect comes, the partial will be done away.

In addition to using the verb *katargeo* in connection with both prophecy and knowledge Paul uses the same form of that verb, the future passive indicative, while he puts *pauo* in the future middle indicative.

> Love never fails;
> but if there are gifts of prophecy, they will be done away
> (*katargeo*; future passive);

if there are tongues, they will cease (*pauo*; future middle);
if there is knowledge, it will be done away (*katargeo*; future passive).
For we know in part and we prophesy in part; but when the perfect comes, the partial will be done away.

The passive voice in Greek functions just like it does in English; it tells us someone or something, an outside agent, acts on the subject to cause the result. In English we usually form the passive by adding words like was or will be (the fence will be painted), while in Greek they add specific endings to the verb. In this verse we learn that an outside cause will stop the gifts of prophecy and knowledge. They will be done away, the form of the Greek verb telling us that someone or something will cause the end of those spiritual gifts.

The middle voice that Paul uses in regard to the end of tongues doesn't have an equivalent in English, but its normal function is what the term *middle* suggests. It falls between the active ("I slept") and the passive ("I was put to sleep"). It's sometimes called the reflexive case, and in our example it would mean something like "I fell asleep." The Greek middle voice can carry different meanings depending in the specific verb, but the most common sense is that the action happened not because the subject directed it or another agent caused it, but that it happened in the natural course of things. Thus, Paul says that whereas the gifts of prophecy and knowledge will be stopped, the gift of tongues will end.

In verses 9-10 Paul writes more about these gifts but only two of the three, knowledge and prophecy. "For we know in part and we prophesy in part; but when the perfect comes, the partial will be done away" (vv. 9-10). As you probably anticipated, and as the NASB indicates, in verse 10 he uses the same verb, *katargeo*, in the same form (future passive indicative), as he did in verse 8 to describe the cessation of these two gifts.

What outside agent causes these two miraculous gifts to end—and why? Paul never answers the first question but ties their withdrawal to the arrival of "the perfect." The fact Paul doesn't go into more detail about what that perfect thing is suggests the Corinthians knew what he meant but once again we have to look closely at the details of the Greek to get the answer.

Like most languages Greek has separate masculine, feminine, and neuter forms for nouns, pronouns, articles, and verbs. Paul chose the neuter form for the perfect in verse 10, indicating that the cause for the end of knowledge and prophecy is a thing, not a person. The Greek could be accurately translated, "When that which is perfect comes," but not, "When he who is perfect comes." That is, those gifts are not withdrawn when Christ returns as some suggest. Paul would never use the neuter form to refer to the Person of Christ. This leads us to ask what *thing* is perfect. The answer is the completed Word of God.

James writes that anyone who "looks into the perfect law, the law of liberty" and also obeys it will be blessed in his doing (James 1:25). He uses the same word for *perfect* here that Paul chose in 1 Corinthians 13:10.

The writers of the New Testament understood that they spoke with authority and that their writings qualified as Scripture. In 2 Peter 3:15-16 Peter uses the word Scripture to describe Paul's writings and Paul clearly intends his teachings to be received as authoritative. For an example see 1 Corinthians 7:10-12 where Paul first cites instructions Christ gave while on earth and then gives his own instructions, which he intends to be received with equal authority.

The Scriptures were written under the direct and controlling influence of the Holy Spirit (2 Peter 1:21). They are God-breathed and thoroughly equip the believer for every good work (2 Tim. 3:16-17). But until the New Testament was completed, individual believers and churches didn't have all the instruction needed to do God's will in the world. Thus, God gave individuals the gifts of prophecy and knowledge. The person with the gift of prophecy received a supernatural communication directly from God to deliver to others. The gift of knowledge was the possession of information that could not be known through natural means and had been given to the individual by God. Nathan knew that David had arranged for the death of Uriah (2 Sam. 12:7) and Peter demonstrated this gift when he accused Ananias of withholding some of the money from the sale of his property (Acts 5:1-4).

God used these two miraculous gifts, prophecy and knowledge, to communicate his will until the time the perfect Word of God was completed. For this reason they are sometimes referred to as revelatory gifts; they were the means by which God revealed his will. But now the perfect has come and once the Word of God was completed near the end of the first century God withdrew the revelatory gifts. When the perfect came the gifts of prophecy and knowledge were stopped.

It's interesting to note that in 1 Corinthians 13 Paul specifies the circumstances under which the two revelatory gifts would be withdrawn but gives no further information about the ending of tongues. That's because he discusses tongues, a particular problem in that church, in chapter 14 explaining why they will come to an end.

We need to remember that the gift of tongues was the miraculous ability to speak in an existing language unknown to the speaker (see chapter 8 in Understanding Your Bible). In 1 Corinthians 14:22 Paul describes the gift of tongues as a sign for unbelievers and in 1:22 he wrote that Jews require signs. Thus the sign gifts, including tongues, were given to the church for the sake of unbelieving Jews to accredit the preaching of Christ's atonement and the equality of Jews and Gentiles in this new dispensation. The goal was, as Paul wrote in Romans 11:14, "to make my fellow Jews jealous, and thus save some of them."

Again we note that Paul discusses tongues only in 1 Corinthians, a letter written to a church with a strong Jewish history located next door to the synagogue. That's not to say it was the only location where miraculous sign gifts appeared, but this setting illustrates their purpose. During a transitional period the miraculous signs that Jews require were done among them, accrediting the message of the gospel.

This explains why Paul used a middle verb to describe the cessation of tongues and not a passive verb as he used with prophecy and knowledge. God didn't act directly to end tongues. They ceased with the end of the transitional period during which the need of the Jews for miraculous signs was accommodated by God.

So we can say that during the second half of the first century two different changes were going on, each involving miraculous gifts. The revelatory gifts, prophecy and knowledge, were stopped (passive verb) by God at the completion of the canon of Scripture. This happened at a specific point in time concurrent with John's completion of Revelation. The sign gifts, given to Israel for the purpose of accreditation, came to an end (middle verb) when God concluded the transition in which he established the validity of the preaching of salvation through Christ and Jew/Gentile equality. This more gradual transition is evident in Paul's statement, "I now go to the Gentiles" spoken by him three times in Acts.

IMPLICATIONS AND APPLICATIONS

The miraculous gifts divide the contemporary church into two groups—those who practice them and those who don't. Our response to a church's use of these gifts differs slightly, depending in part on whether it involves the revelatory gifts of prophecy and knowledge or the sign gifts. The former—prophecy and knowledge—bring serious error in that the speaker claims to deliver revelation direct from God, thus qualifying as a false prophet. The message itself may be ambiguous and harmless enough, but the presumption and potential for harm makes this practice unacceptable.

As we've seen, Paul's use of the sign gifts was temporary, employed during the transition period to accredit his ministry and message before the Jews. This explains why Paul makes no mention of the sign gifts in his later letters, including the three written to Timothy and Ti-

47

tus, who served as pastors. In the Corinthian letters he prepares them for the ending of the sign gifts and minimizes the practice of water baptism.

This requires that we respond carefully when we interact with churches and individuals who believe water baptism and the sign gifts are still part of God's plan for today's believers. In either case the first question is, how central are these practices to someone's view of spiritual health? A church that requires water baptism for membership or service has added a stipulation Paul would have strictly rejected (see 1 Cor. 1:14-17) and has placed an unbiblical barrier within the Body of Christ. That fits within the context of Galatians 5:1-6, where Paul addresses the problem of those who make the Jewish ceremony of circumcision essential. However, a church that simply encourages water baptism as a nonessential step in the Christian life seems to fit within the context of passages like 1 Corinthians 7:18-19, where the practice of another Jewish ceremony is said to be inconsequential.

With regard to the sign gifts, we've seen they ended with the transitional period covered by the book of Acts. What, then, are we to make of the claim of tongues and healings in contemporary churches? As we discussed in Understanding Your Bible, the New Testament practice of tongues meant speaking in a real language unknown to the speaker, something very different than what happens today. Healings today almost always involve ambiguous symptoms and/or unverified outcomes. Does that mean no real miracle ever takes place? Certainly not! God is not limited and sometimes heals through medicine and sometimes through a miraculous answer to intercessory prayers. However, we also note that in 2 Thessalonians 2:9 Paul says the coming of the lawless one "is by the activity of Satan with all power and false signs and wonders." Supernatural events are by definition outside the laws of nature and can be done by God or by Satan (see Ex. 7:20-22). So while most "miracles" performed in churches today can, when examined objectively, be dismissed as inconsistent with the biblical model (speaking in tongues) or not truly miraculous (healings), we

48

must allow for the possibility that the one who opposes God and seeks to lead believers and unbelievers astray is responsible for supernatural activity.

QUESTIONS

1. How does the Bible you normally use translate the verbs in 1 Corinthians 13:8? Does that translation accurately reflect what we learned about the Greek words Paul chose?
2. What are the two revelatory gifts, and what led to their withdrawal by God?
3. Why did Paul practice the sign gifts early in his ministry?
4. How would you explain the practice of those gifts in the contemporary church?

THE GOSPELS
How should we read these four key books of the Bible?

When we understand that this current dispensation and the Body of Christ began with the apostle Paul we're presented with an interesting question. The Gospels record events from the earthly life and ministry of Christ, which took place within the dispensation of Law. Yet all four Gospels were written after the dispensation of Grace began and at least one of them, John, after the point when Paul specifically says Israel has been set aside as God's special people (see Rom. 11:20-22). It's also worth noting that another Gospel writer, Luke, was a Gentile who traveled and worked with Paul on his missionary journeys. If part of good Bible study is paying attention to the dispensational setting of a biblical passage or book, what should we do with the Gospels?

Why would God direct four men to write about the words and actions of Jesus Christ, including his teachings about the coming millennial kingdom after the offer of that kingdom had been withdrawn? How should members of the Body of Christ living 2,000 years later and looking for the rapture understand these four books? What role should they play in the teaching of a local church?

To answer these questions we'll begin with a look at some general guidelines for reading and interpreting the Gospels.

WHAT IS THE BACKGROUND OF EACH GOSPEL?

The Bible contains several categories of literature including history, poetry, and correspondence. Many people think of the Gospels as history because they record events, but they would be better placed in a category of their own because they don't match the characteristics of historical books. Especially when read alongside one another, the Gospels are clearly about much more than presenting historical information regarding the life and work of Christ. Each of the four writers had his own purpose for writing, which governed what material was included and how each Gospel was structured. Only one, Luke, includes a birth narrative, Mark has almost no teaching material, and more than 90 percent of John's content doesn't appear in the other three Gospels. With the exception of Luke the material they contain isn't in chronological order. These books are unlike anything else in the Bible.

Each of the Gospels is arranged around its own theme with content chosen by the author for the way it supports his theme. The first three—Matthew, Mark, and Luke—use much of the same material but in very different ways designed to suit their author's individual purpose. For that reason they are referred to as *synoptics*, a word that means they look at the same things. As noted, John has very little content in common with the other three.

Matthew's Gospel presents Christ as Israel's King, their promised Messiah. He emphasizes that theme in several ways, including beginning with a genealogy that traces Christ's lineage back to Abraham with a focus on David (see Matt. 1:1,6,17). Joseph is identified as a "son of David" (Matt. 1:20), only Matthew records the visit of the wise men who ask, "Where is he who is born king of the Jews?" (2:2), and he uses the words king and kingdom more than any of the other three. Matthew refers to the Old Testament prophecies about the coming Messiah more than 60 times, more than any of the other Gospel writers.

Another interesting feature of Matthew's Gospel is his arrangement of the material. He organizes his content into blocks, alternating between five sections of narrative material that record Christ's actions with five sections recording his teachings, followed by the passion narrative. Within each block the content is grouped thematically, with miracles placed together in chapters eight and nine and parables in chapter 13. What we call the Sermon on the Mount was probably several separate teaching sessions given at various times but placed here by Matthew in a way that made it easier for his readers to remember. These and other characteristics suggest that Matthew wrote his Gospel for Jewish believers probably in or near Judea so they could defend their faith in Jesus as the promised Messiah. He often structures his content in a way to make it easier for them to memorize, like arranging his genealogy into three sections of 14 generations each (Matt. 1:17). All this would help early Jewish believers as they respond to the charge of heresy from their countrymen.

Mark focuses on Christ as a suffering servant and many of his narratives emphasize Christ's emotions including sorrow and compassion. Mark has no birth narrative because a servant's birth isn't noteworthy. He focuses on Christ's miracles with almost nothing of his teaching because a servant is known for what he does, not what he says. Mark uses the word immediately more than all the other Gospels combined in order to emphasize Christ's busyness as he moves from one action to the next. The suffering of Christ gets special attention with more than 40 percent of the Gospel devoted to the events of the last week and his crucifixion.

Just as Matthew's Gospel is associated with Judea, Mark's Gospel seems to have originated in Rome. He uses Latin words to explain the meaning of Greek words (Mk. 12:42; 15:16) and Mark alone includes the detail that Simon of Cyrene, the father of Alexander and Rufus, was the one forced to carry Christ's cross on the way to Golgotha. This fits with Romans 16:13 where Paul sends greetings to Rufus and his mother in Rome. Peter spent his final years in Rome and was eventually put to death there. In 1 Peter 5:13 he writes that "Mark, my son" was there with him. Many have seen the input of Peter as an eye witness in some of the details that Mark records including the emotions Christ felt at key points in his ministry.

Luke's Gospel is unique in many respects including that it was written for an individual, Theophilus, and pairs with the Book of Acts in which Luke continues the chronology of events after the ascension. Luke was also the only Gentile to write one of the Gospels and may have been the only one to have not witnessed any of the events. (Many think that Mark 14:51-52 is autobiographical, putting Mark in that scene.) In his prologue Luke says his intent is to write an orderly account (1:3), an expression in Greek that refers to a chronological account and distinguishes it from Matthew's thematic arrangement.

Luke, a Gentile, writes an account of Christ's ministry for another Gentile, Theophilus, and emphasizes the humanity of Christ. Luke alone gives us the birth narrative, includes a genealogy that traces Christ back to Adam, and records details about his humanity, including personal and social growth. Luke records Christ's contact with women and the poor, whom he refers to as often as Matthew and Mark combined. Only Luke refers to Christ as Savior, a term that emphasizes his relationship to humanity.

John, as already noted, records different material with 92 percent of the content unique to his Gospel. John's Gospel focuses on the deity of Christ with less emphasis on his humanity. The prologue (1:1-18) sets the theme for the book and John repeatedly brings up the preexistence of Christ. Christ performs signs that prove his divine origin (see 2:11; 3:2; 20:30-31) and the many private conversations John records, like that with Nicodemus and the Samaritan woman, emphasize Christ's deity.

Features of John's Gospel include a clear statement about his purpose for writing, something that must be inferred with the Synoptics. (We need to ask why Luke thought Theophilus needed the "orderly account he refers to in Lk. 1:3.) In 20:31 John writes, "...these are written so that you may believe that Jesus is the Christ, the Son of God, and that by believing you may have life in his name." John's theme is the deity of Christ, and his purpose was evangelistic. Therefore, his readers were nonbelievers, probably Jewish (Jesus is the Christ, the Messiah), and probably living in the area of Ephesus where John spent his final years.

Thus we see that the Gospels, even the three Synoptics, are each unique in their characteristics and theme. Three of them—Matthew, Mark, and John—seem to be written for Jewish readers, while Luke was addressed to the Gentile Theophilus. Matthew stresses Christ's fulfillment of the prophecies about the coming Messiah, and John refers 17 times to the miraculous signs Christ did that confirm his deity, a dynamic Paul writes is particularly Jewish (1 Cor. 1:22). Yet each of them was written after the beginning of the Body of Christ, and two of the authors, Mark and Luke, worked with Paul during his ministry (see Col. 4:10 and 2 Tim. 4:11).

IMPLICATIONS AND APPLICATIONS

First, we reaffirm what we stated above, that 2 Timothy 3:16-17 teaches us no portion of Scripture should be viewed as unnecessary or irrelevant. It is all equally inspired and equally designed to equip us for every good work. The loss of any passage of the Bible, including through intentional disregard, limits God's intended work in the life of the believer. For this reason alone we should spend time reading and learning from the Gospels.

But the fact that God chose these particular men to write the Gospel accounts causes us to consider additional reasons for paying close attention to them. God could have chosen anyone to write the Gospel accounts at any time and under any circumstances. That his sovereign will directed a Gentile coworker with Paul (Luke) and another fellow traveler and coworker (Mark) tells us these Gospels have very direct relevance and significance for those within the dispensation of

56

Grace, and that the teachings on the millennial kingdom have applicability to us.

Mark and John each brought to their Gospel memories from three years spent with Christ during his public ministry. Their eye witness accounts provide us with an invaluable resource for understanding the incarnation, the most significant event in human history. The fact their accounts are so different only adds to their value.

Knowing the background and perspective of each of these four men only increases the impact their contribution to Scripture can have as we seek to read and understand. Too many Christians think the Gospels, especially the synoptics, cover the same material in the same way. To the contrary, understanding the unique background and perspective of these four men helps us see the differences in their accounts and increases our benefit from spending time in this crucial portion of Scripture.

QUESTIONS

1. Give the basic background information for each of the four Gospels, including the author's background and the theme of each.
2. Why do you think God chose a Gentile to write one of the Gospels?
3. Using whatever resources you have available, can you identify the theme of each Gospel and how that theme is presented?

WHAT IS THE DISPENSATIONAL POSITION OF THE GOSPELS?

This information about authorship makes answering the question of the Gospels' dispensational position interesting. The easiest solution is to say that because of their content they belong within the dispensation of Law and should be understood in the same way we read the majority of the Old Testament. This approach has perhaps been the most common among mid-Acts dispensationalists, but it fails to adequately take into account several features we've just noted:

- The Gospel of Luke was written by a Gentile who traveled with Paul on two of his missionary journeys and who was with him during his first Roman imprisonment. Regardless of how we understand the issue of the dispensational position of believers from the period before Paul's ministry, Luke was clearly a member of the Body of Christ.

- The Gospel of Mark was written by someone who accompanied Paul and Barnabas as they left for their first missionary journey and was recommended to the Colossian church (Col. 4:10). Paul wanted Mark with him as he faced death in Rome because, "He is very useful to me" (2 Tim. 4:11).

- The Gospel of John was written around AD 90 well after Paul's statement in Romans 11:21-22 that Israel had been set aside.

- All four gospels were written after Paul received the revelation of the mystery of Jew/Gentile equality, which, as we discussed in the previous section of this book, resulted in those who were believers prior to that point becoming members of the Body of Christ.

These factors require us to take a more careful look at how we read and understand the Gospels from a dispensational standpoint. The historical setting of these four books, Christ's earthly ministry, falls within the dispensation of Law, and as we'll see, at least a large portion of the content has to do with Israel's future as God's special people, including his return to establish their promised messianic kingdom. So how do we harmonize that with the background features noted above?

Perhaps the first step involves remembering how central the Person and work of Christ are to every aspect of our faith. When thinking back to his early ministry to the Corinthians Paul wrote, "For I decided to know nothing among you except Jesus Christ and him crucified" (1 Cor. 2:2). We know from the Book of Acts that Paul's pattern when entering a new city was to go into the synagogue to talk with the Jews about Christ. Six times Acts says he "reasoned" with the Jews, which certainly would have involved the use of Old Testament prophecies and their fulfillment in Christ's earthly ministry (see Acts 17:2). The record of Paul's address to the Jews at the synagogue in Antioch (Acts 13:16-41) reads very much like an abbreviated version of Matthew's presentation of Jesus as the Messiah. Both show from the Old Testament the thread of events and prophecies that point forward to Jesus. The theme of Matthew's Gospel—that all the evidence shows Jesus was the promised Messiah and his crucifixion was the fulfillment of prophesy—has critical relevance to Jewish evangelism. It also strengthens the faith of Jewish believers under opposition from their countrymen. In that regard the Gospel of Matthew remains relevant today.

The Gospel of Matthew teaches contemporary believers, including Gentile Christians, that the Jesus who is our Savior was the One the prophets promised. Christianity is not a new religion based on a founder who appeared 2,000 year ago out of nowhere. Ours is a faith with roots in the prophecies and promises of the Old Testament about God's plan for mankind's salvation.

Mark's emphasis on Christ's life of service and suffering aligns with Paul's comments in Philippians 2:5-8, where he draws on the pattern Christ's life set for us, a reference that only works if his readers were familiar with the details of Christ's life and ministry. Nine times Paul describes himself as a servant and ten times refers to his own suffering, including connecting them to the sufferings of Christ (Phil. 3:10). Mark's Gospel originated in Rome where more than 80 percent of the population were slaves, a percentage probably reflected in the local church there. So Mark's point of emphasis in his Gospel and Paul's view of the Christian walk align closely and teach us how we are to view the Christian life (1 Cor. 11:1).

Luke's Gospel stressing the humanity of Christ addresses a major theological issue that has always been a problem for some both inside and outside the church. The substitutionary death of Christ is only effective if he was fully man. But perhaps the most important thing to remember in this context is that Luke's Gospel is volume one, followed by the Book of Acts, both addressed to Theophilus. Taken together they provide a continuous narrative of the entry and spread of the gospel of salvation. Luke tells Theophilus he's doing this to provide "certainty concerning the things you have been taught" (Acts 1:4). That interesting phrase suggests that Theophilus was either an unbeliever carefully exploring the claims of the gospel or a relatively new believer seeking to better understand his faith. Either way, Luke realized how important it was for Theophilus to have a grasp of the historical events that extend from the birth of Jesus Christ to Paul's arrival in Rome including the dispensational transition that took place during the time covered by these two volumes. We certainly benefit from the same historical perspective.

John's emphasis on the deity of Christ is equally essential to any understanding of the gospel. By the end of the first century a significant heresy now known as Gnosticism was arising that denied the full deity of Christ, viewing him instead as a created being. John's opening words make his point of emphasis in his Gospel very clear (see 1:1-3), and his statement about his evangelistic purpose for writing (20:30) shows the connection between the deity of Christ and saving faith. John's record of Christ's words and deeds continues to be an effective tool for communicating the gospel.

Besides these very practical reasons for knowing the content of each Gospel there is an additional even greater benefit to reading the Gospels. We live in an age increasingly characterized by a self-centeredness that seems to have as its motto, "It's all about me." Information, merchandise, and organizations are all geared to meet the specific desires of each individual. Technology allows marketers and social media to send us content specifically targeted to our unique interests, reinforcing a sense of our own importance.

Immediacy is another defining characteristic of our culture. The speed at which information and communication happen has the effect of shortening our perspective. Last week's news is old, and anything from five years ago is obsolete and irrelevant. The rate at which things change has us convinced the "new" is both improved and a must-have. Most of us have trouble remembering what happened last year because we're overcome with the vast amount of information we receive from around the world regarding what happened yesterday. Our ancestors measured change by the generation and we measure it by the month.

The Gospels give us the perfect antidote, reminding us that all of human history is his story, and that God's sovereign plan overrides all others. These four books show that Christ's first coming was the fulfillment of God's plan since before time and his second coming will be the climax of the course of events that he controls in specific detail. He "works all things after the counsel of his will" (Eph. 1:11) and all the glory is his. God is sovereign over the kingdoms of men (Ps. 103:19) and his plan will all come to pass (Is. 55:11).

The Gospels should be read not as just about a particular 33-year period, but as a presentation of one very significant stage in the outworking of God's eternal purpose, as part of a much bigger picture. The redemption provided through Christ's first coming and his teaching about the messianic kingdom at his second coming remind us that while we too often get caught up in our immediate circumstances, God is working his plan that spans all of human history. His great work from before the beginning of time to beyond the end of human history provides us with a needed sense of perspective.

All of this leads us to conclude that the Gospels have an important role to play for believers in this dispensation. If we removed these four books from the Bible the rest of the New Testament would make no sense and Paul's many references to the life and example of Christ would lose their impact. We also need and can receive great benefit from the words and actions of the incarnate Christ as we seek to live godly lives in this present age (Titus 2:11).

What then are we to do with the material in the Gospels that so clearly and specifically speaks to God's special relationship with Israel under the dispensation of Law and his prophetic agenda for the Jews?

The first step is to note Paul's statement in 2 Timothy 3:16, "All Scripture is inspired by God and profitable for teaching, for reproof, for correction, for training in righteousness." Any approach to the Bible that ignores the Gospels or relegates them to a secondary role misunderstands their background as noted above but, more importantly, ignores Paul's instruction about the whole of Scripture. Paul told the Ephesian elders that, "I did not shrink from declaring to you the whole purpose of God" (Acts 20:27). Certainly God's plan for the consummation of history fits within that description. To suggest that there is lesser value to reading the Gospels diminishes the work of the Holy Spirit in applying Scripture to the believer's life so that "...the man of God may be adequate, equipped for every good work" (2 Tim. 3:17).

Another key to properly reading the Gospels is distinguishing between interpretation and application. The former term refers to God's intent when he inspired the human author of any given section of Scripture. A particular passage has only one interpretation, one meaning, and that is the one God intended. A common and dangerous error when discussing the Bible is the use of expressions like, "To me this passage means...." That suggests the section being discussed could have a different, equally legitimate meaning to someone else. God inspired the human authors to write the very words that best communicated the truth he wanted us to receive. Our sometimes difficult task is to use every resource available to us to discern that truth. In addition to seeking the Holy Spirit's wisdom, interpretation may require looking at the verses in the original language, learning the cultural and historic setting of a particular passage, and reading trustworthy commentaries. Through these means we can learn what the author meant and what the Author wants us to learn.

Only after arriving at a particular passage's one interpretation can we ask, "How does this apply to me?" This step must come after determining the interpretation to ensure it is consistent with that interpretation. When this methodology is applied to the content of the Gospels we begin by asking, in the case of his teachings, "What truth did Christ intend to communicate in this section?" Or, when reading one of the narrative sections, "What divine truth does God want us to learn from this incident?" Once the interpretation has been identified we must ask how that truth should impact daily life. While interpretation comes first, the step of application is necessary to fulfill the dynamic Paul talks about in 2 Timothy 3:16-17, where he tells us all Scripture is profitable so we can be equipped for every good work. If we ignore the Gospels we cannot be thoroughly equipped.

IMPLICATIONS AND APPLICATIONS

It is a mistake to think that because we are not part of Israel or God's plan and agenda for that nation that the millennial kingdom promised to Israel has no bearing or significance for us. Correcting this notion starts with our view of human history.

Human government is a divinely established social institution that, like marriage and the family, extends across time and history. Every day we see how each of those institutions has been corrupted by sin with disastrous results for individuals and societies. For that reason Psalm 146:3 reminds us, "Do not trust in princes, in mortal man, in whom there is no salvation." In every era, in all locations, and in every form of government we see corruption from rulers who seek their own benefit, not justice and the benefit of their people. As a result we experience horrible wars, exploitation, injustice, and state-sanctioned immorality. These great evils are not what God intended or designed. They are instead the predictable outcomes of the universal affliction of sin.

The Bible is the story of God's victory over sin and its effects, from the eternal death sentence on individuals (1 Cor. 15:54-57) to the corruption seen in society. Just as Christ's first coming brought individual salvation, so his second coming will restore society to God's intent and design. Isaiah speaks about this aspect of the millennial kingdom often, including in Isaiah 11 where the prophet speaks about the coming of Messiah: "There shall come forth a shoot from the stump of Jesse, and a branch from his roots shall bear fruit. And his delight shall be in the fear of the Lord. He shall not judge by what his eyes see, or decide disputes by what his ears hear, but with righteousness he shall judge the poor, and decide with equity for the meek of the earth. Righteousness shall be the belt of his waist, and faithfulness the belt of his loins" (vv. 1, 3-5). In Isaiah 16:5 we read: "A throne will even be established in lovingkindness, and a judge will sit on it in faithfulness in the tent of David; Moreover, he will seek justice and be prompt in righteousness." David writes, "And he will judge the world in righteousness, he will execute judgment for the peoples with equity" (Ps. 9:8).

Mid-Acts dispensationalists should read with joy and reverence the Gospels' birth narratives and the accounts of Christ's crucifixion and resurrection because we see one of history's great victories, namely the defeat of sin and the condemnation it brought to every person. God broke into history and graciously brought life, eternal and abundant. In the same way Christ's second coming will bring victory over the horrible effects of sin in society as he rules in peace and with perfect justice.

Furthermore, Christ's teachings give us instructions on righteousness in daily living, including our relationships with others and the state. If we truly grieve about the evils of this world, members of the

Body of Christ should look forward with eager anticipation to Messiah's earthly reign.

QUESTIONS

1. Identify at least two reasons we should read and study the Gospels.
2. Name the theme of each of the gospels and one way in which that author develops it.
3. What can you do to increase your knowledge of the Gospels?

A KEY WORD

In the process of discovering the interpretation of many Gospel passages and their dispensational position we need to understand the meaning of the word kingdom in these books. That word is used by many biblical authors in a variety of ways, so we need to pay careful attention to the context of each. Comparing examples of how the word kingdom is used throughout Scripture shows several categories of meaning.

In Psalm 22:28 David writes, "For the kingdom is the Lord's, and he rules over the nations." In this verse we're reminded that God is the sovereign ruler of all creation and his rule extends through all time and every dimension. Psalm 45:6 says, "Your throne, O God, is forever and ever; a scepter of uprightness is the scepter of your kingdom." We can call this God's universal kingdom because it covers all things at all times. "Your kingdom is an everlasting kingdom. And your dominion endures throughout all generations" (Ps. 145:13).

In 1 Samuel 28:17 Saul is told, "The Lord has torn the kingdom out of your hand and given it to your neighbor, to David." This passage clearly refers to the nation of Israel as formed at Sinai and later constituted as a monarchy with Saul as its first king. Perhaps the majority of uses of the word kingdom in the Old Testament refer to a political kingdom, whether that of Israel or one of the other nations in the area. "I commanded Joshua at that time, saying, 'Your eyes have seen all that the Lord your God has done to these two kings; so the Lord shall do to all the kingdoms into which you are about to cross'" (Deut. 3:21). Isaiah prays, "Now, O Lord our God, deliver us from his hand that all the kingdoms of the earth may know that you alone, Lord, are God" (Isa. 37:20). Three times in Daniel 4 we read that God is sovereign over the kingdoms on earth (vv. 17, 25, 32), another example of the word kingdom used to describe political entities on earth.

Paul uses the word *kingdom* 14 times in his letters with at least two different meanings. In Colossians 1:13 he writes, "For he rescued us from the domain of darkness, and transferred us to the kingdom of his beloved Son." Paul uses a form of the verb *transferred* that refers to an action completed in the past, showing that we were formerly outside, in the domain of darkness (see Eph. 2:1), but with our salvation we have been placed within the kingdom of his Son. What we will call the *spiritual kingdom* includes those who belong to Christ through faith and encompasses God's work in and through these believers. In Romans 14:17 Paul writes, "For the kingdom of God is not eating and drinking, but righteousness and peace and joy in the Holy Spirit." This spiritual kingdom is probably also Paul's intent in 1 Corinthians 4:20 where, when warning the members of that troublesome church about his impending visit, he writes, "For the kingdom of God does not consist in words but in power." In Colossians 4 Paul refers to three individuals as "the only fellow workers for the kingdom of God who are from the circumcision" (v. 11).

Paul also talks about a kingdom that is in the future. The Greek word for *last* is *eschatos*, and the division of theology that deals with the last events in human history is called eschatology, so we can call it the *eschatological kingdom.* In 1 Corinthians 6:9 Paul writes, "Or do you not know that the unrighteous will not inherit the kingdom of God?" Galatians 5:21 says, "...those who practice such things will not inherit the kingdom of God." Paul tells Timothy that the Lord, "will bring me safely to his heavenly kingdom; to him be the glory forever and ever. Amen" (2 Tim. 4:18). Thus, this kingdom is still in the future and only for believers. This eschatological kingdom is probably also Paul's meaning in 1 Thessalonians 2:12 and 2 Thessalonians 1:5.

A fifth usage of the word *kingdom* appears in the prophets and refers to the coming of Israel's Messiah, who will reign on David's throne. Isaiah 9:7 says, "There will be no end to the increase of his government or of peace, on the throne of David and over his kingdom, to establish it and to uphold it with justice and righteousness from then on and forevermore. The zeal of the Lord of hosts will accomplish this." Micah predicts an age of peace when the nations will beat their swords into plowshares, never again training for war, and the lame and outcasts will be lifted up (Micah 4:3, 6-7). "As for you, tower of the flock, hill of the daughter of Zion, to you it will come, even the former dominion will come, the kingdom of the daughter of Jerusalem" (4:8). Micah here prophecies that the nation of Israel, currently weak and under attack, will be restored to the glory of David's reign.

Other well-known passages, though they do not include the word *kingdom*, clearly refer to the future reign of Christ over all the earth from Jerusalem. Isaiah 11 describes Messiah's righteousness and his rule over the nations and the restoration of the remnant of Israel "from the four corners of the earth" (11:12). Zechariah 14 prophecies a great attack on Israel and Jerusalem that is only overcome by the arrival of the Lord who will appear on the Mount of Olives (14:4) and bring deliverance. Following that great victory, "the Lord will be king over all the earth; in that day the Lord will be the only one, and his name the only one" (v. 9).

Revelation 19:11-21 also describes this attack on Israel and the deliverance Messiah brings at his arrival. In 20:3 we're told that Satan is bound and Christ reigns for 1,000 years, and "after these things he (Satan) must be released for a short time." For this reason the reign of Christ is referred to the *millennial kingdom*.

Is there a difference between Paul's eschatological kingdom and the millennial kingdom? Paul describes the former as being both future and made of all the redeemed, including himself (2 Tim. 4:18). The millennial kingdom is also future but the participants are those who are alive on earth at the time of Christ's second coming and the resurrected righteous martyrs of the tribulation (Rev. 20:4). Thus, while both Paul's eschatological kingdom and the millennial kingdom are future, they seem distinct.

We'll discuss some of these kingdoms in more detail in the section on eschatology including what, if any, overlap there may be between them. At this point, in order to better understand the Gospels and their relevance for believers in the dispensation of Grace, we need to determine how the word *kingdom* is used in these four books, where it appears 119 times. Christ tells his disciples that the kingdom is near ("at hand"), gives parables to teach about the kingdom, and he speaks about those who will enter the kingdom.

Since so much of what Christ says about the kingdom refers to the arrival of that kingdom at some point in the future we can conclude he is not talking about God's universal kingdom or an existing political kingdom. For the same reason we can eliminate the spiritual kingdom Paul speaks about. That kingdom is present currently and is unseen whereas the one Christ speaks about will have a visible and physical presence when it arrives (see Matt. 6:10; 8:11). That leaves the possibilities that Christ used the word *kingdom* in the same sense as Paul's eschatological kingdom, as Israel's millennial kingdom, or with some different additional meaning.

Perhaps the best way to identify the meaning behind the word *kingdom* in the Gospels is by looking at an appearance of the word outside those four books. In Acts 1 Luke continues the narrative of his Gospel with an account of the ascension. As they stood on the Mount of Olives just east of Jerusalem 40 days after the resurrection, the disciples asked Christ, "Lord, is it at this time you are restoring the kingdom to Israel?" (v. 6). Having spent three years with Christ listening to his teaching about the kingdom, we can assume they used the word *kingdom* here in the same way they understood him to use it during that time. If their question indicated they had somehow misunderstood his use of the word we should expect him to correct their error. Instead, he says, "It is not for you to know times or epochs which the Father has fixed by his own authority" (v. 7). While he doesn't answer their question about the timing of the restoration of the kingdom, he also doesn't challenge their understanding of his use of the word over the previous three years.

70

We thus conclude that Christ's use of the word kingdom refers to the promised future millennial kingdom when Messiah will rule over the earth from Jerusalem on the throne of David. The Twelve believed Jesus was the Messiah and had expected him to set up the kingdom promised by the prophets. Instead, he died the humiliating death of crucifixion, leaving them dejected and disillusioned. Three days later he surprised them again by rising from the dead, which renewed their hopes for the kingdom promised by the prophets. This led to their question on the Mount of Olives. "Is this it? Is now the time?" Behind their question lies the roller coaster of emotions they've felt over the last seven weeks and their realization that if they got it wrong before they shouldn't assume anything even at this point.

No sooner had he given them a response that wasn't an answer than he ascended and disappeared from their sight. We have to sympathize with these men who, having had their hopes dashed at Golgotha and then raised again at the resurrection, now watched the basis of their hopes disappear from them. One moment they ask in hopeful expectation, "Is now the time?" and the next moment he disappears into heaven. Their amazement must have been mixed with confusion and yet more disappointment.

Suddenly two men in white clothing appeared and said, "Men of Galilee, why do you stand looking into the sky? This Jesus, who has been taken up from you into heaven, will come in just the same way as you have watched him go into heaven" (v. 11). With no reference to the timing of that return we can probably assume that the disciples inferred he would come back in the very near future, particularly because just before ascending Christ told them "not to leave Jerusalem, but to wait for what the Father had promised" (v. 4).

The disciples were probably also very familiar with Zechariah 14:4, "In that day his feet will stand on the Mount of Olives, which is in front of Jerusalem on the east." At that moment the Twelve stood on the Mount of Olives, having just watched the Messiah ascend to heaven, and were then told he would return "in just the same way as you have watched him go into heaven." Once again their roller coaster of emotions have gone from a high to a low, and then back up again.

Understanding the use of the word kingdom in the Gospels as referring to the millennial kingdom promised to Israel guides us as we seek the interpretation of any particular Gospel passage. The series of parables in Matthew 13 about the kingdom are thus to be understood as preparing Christ's followers for the arrival of their great hope. "Your kingdom come" (Matt. 6:10) should be interpreted the same way.

Many contemporary authors and preachers interpret the references to the kingdom in the Gospels as a reference to something similar to the spiritual kingdom Paul refers to and of which all believers are members. They do so based on Luke 17:21, "For behold, the kingdom of God is in your midst." The relatively rare preposition "in" used in this verse can mean either among you or inside you. This leads some to conclude Christ's many references to the kingdom are not to a future millennial kingdom set up by the returning Messiah but a more important spiritual kingdom located within believers.

This interpretation of the word *kingdom* in the Gospels as a reference only to an internal spiritual kingdom then determines their interpretation of much of Christ's teaching including the parables of the kingdom. Instead of having an eschatological focus on Christ's future return, his kingdom teachings should, this view maintains, be understood to teach truths about the daily walk and mindset of all believers.

However, the broader context of Luke 17:21 indicates that Christ's meaning was "in your midst." He emphasized that the one speaking to them was the hoped-for Messiah who would return to establish the promised millennial kingdom.

The Pharisees had asked when the kingdom was coming (v. 20) and Christ responded that it would not arrive with readily observable warning signs appearing ahead of time. Instead, it will arrive suddenly, like the flood that overtook an unsuspecting population in Noah's time, and the destruction that came on Sodom without warning (vv.

22-37). So Christ's response to the Pharisees that the kingdom was "in our midst" was another statement that he was the Messiah who would set up the kingdom that would come suddenly and with judgment.

All this is important because, with the understanding that the word *kingdom* in the Gospels refers to the future millennial reign of Messiah over the world from Jerusalem, we ask why we have four accounts written by members of the Body of Christ in the dispensation of Grace that contain so much teaching on Israel's great hope. If the kingdom the Gospel authors write about is something parallel to Paul's spiritual kingdom, internal and spiritual, there's no conflict. But because the ultimate hope for the Body of Christ is the rapture (see the section on eschatology) this teaching on the kingdom seems almost unnecessary and irrelevant.

IMPLICATIONS AND APPLICATIONS

Even more than the prophets, the four Gospel authors describe how the millennial kingdom will arrive and what it will look like. In his teaching Christ set it against the corrupt rule of Israel's leaders, both secular and religious, who ruled over the people in self-serving hypocrisy. His indictment of Israel's leaders was both a description of sin's effects on societal leadership and, by contrast, a prediction of things under Messiah's rule. Christ gave instructions on what righteous living and godly social relationships look like.

It is certainly true that the disciples looked for the coming kingdom primarily for the political and military restoration it would bring to Israel. But any careful reading of Christ's teachings finds these dimensions and Israel's superiority almost entirely absent from his descriptions of his return and rule. He focused on the spiritual and moral dimensions of the kingdom, both at the individual and the societal level.

The millennial kingdom was promised to Israel and will be centered in Jerusalem, ruled over by the Son of David. But it will be given to the world. Christ's reign on earth will bring blessing to all mankind.

Thus, it is not "Israel's messianic kingdom," but the kingdom that brings unprecedented peace and blessing to all peoples of the earth.

Mid-Acts dispensationalists may be inclined to place a wall between the Gospels and Paul's epistles and view those four books as something like foreign territory with little or no value for the believer in the dispensation of Grace. As we've seen, this perspective fails to take into account the authorship and background of these books. Additionally, the Gospels show us what God's design for individual and social life looks like as he calls Israel to prepare for the kingdom that is near ("at hand"). The moral principles and values of Christ's teachings are not vertical, not specific to the millennial kingdom, but descriptive of what righteousness looks like across all areas of life.

Again, in the section on eschatology we will discuss issues related to Christ's return to establish the millennial kingdom and what part, if any, believers from other dispensations will have in that kingdom and its arrival. But at this point we can say that Christ's teachings about the moral and spiritual characteristics of that time reflect God's design for righteous people in any age. As such they have real value for those who desire to live "sensibly, righteously, and godly in the present age" (Titus 2:12).

Thus, there are several important reasons we should spend time in the Gospels:

- As part of Scripture they are equal to all other portions of the Bible—inspired, inerrant, and profitable (2 Tim. 3:16-17).
- The teaching sections that focus on the return of Christ to establish the millennial kingdom demonstrate God's absolute sovereignty over history and his ultimate victory. They remind us that God is in control of all events and that human history will conform to his plan. Regardless of what our participation may be in those events we should rejoice in these predictions of the victory of our Lord within history.

- The sections about the coming kingdom also teach us that no matter what it looks like in the short term, history is not stumbling along from one chaotic event to the next. God has a great plan, and human history will reach its climax with the presence of Christ ruling on earth with perfect peace and righteousness. Like the Twelve we wonder about the timing of the unfolding, but the Gospels remind us God is at work, and just as the promises of his first coming were fulfilled, so too will the promises of his great kingdom on earth.

- Perhaps most important, the narrative sections clearly show us what righteous living looks like in the presence of sin and a hostile environment. The individual and societal effects of sin haven't changed over the centuries, and neither have the evidences of godly living. The priorities, attitudes, and behaviors Christ modeled and called his disciples to exhibit are timeless characteristics of believers in any age or dispensation.

QUESTIONS

1. Name the ways the word kingdom is used in the Bible and an example of each.
2. How should we understand that word as it's used in the Gospels? Explain your answer.
3. How do you think the average Christian understands the word kingdom as it's used in the Gospels?

ESCHATOLOGY
What does the Bible say about future events?

God in his grace has given us information about his plan for our future. Human nature wants all the details, but in his wisdom God provided only a broad outline of the events that will bring history to a close and usher in eternity. The study of this area of theology is called eschatology, from the Greek word, eschatos, which means last. Thus, eschatology is the study of last things. Perhaps more than any other area of theology this one is most affected by the differing perspectives of Covenant theology and dispensationalism. The basics of these differences have been covered in Understanding Your Bible, so here we will discuss some of the issues and questions that arise when we look at the Bible's teaching about the future from a mid-Acts dispensational perspective.

Since the Bible doesn't give us as much detail as we'd like there are some questions we can't answer with certainty but can only suggest a likely solution based on what Scripture does say. This means students of the Word, even within mid-Acts dispensationalism, will come to different conclusions. We must see this as an acceptable outcome and readily agree to disagree. If the answers were critical and essential to orthodoxy God would have settled the question with clear instruction. The fact he didn't reminds us to keep discourse on these matters at the level of thought-provoking discussion, not line drawing. Thinking and talking about spiritual things is always worthwhile because it causes us to dig into the Bible, which usually causes us to learn more about God's Word. But no matter how convinced we are that our understanding of an issue is correct, if the Bible isn't explicit we must graciously accept believers who come to different conclusions.

The gap between what the Bible tells us about the future and our desire for details is so big, that this section will only address a few of the more basic questions. These have been chosen because they impact our understanding of
other key issues, because they are areas of frequent misunderstanding, or because they just present an interesting topic for consideration not often discussed. Our ability to answer these questions with firm scriptural support will vary, ranging from near certainty to no clear resolution. But in each case, if our work takes us into God's Word with open hearts and minds the effort will bear fruit, even if it doesn't provide clear answers.

WHAT DOES THE BIBLE TEACH ABOUT THE RAPTURE?

As discussed in Understanding Your Bible, the dispensation of Grace climaxes with the event known as the rapture. The first question concerning what the Bible teaches about the rapture has to do with its timing. This touches on two related issues: the date for the rapture and its place relative to other events on the biblical timeline, specifically the tribulation. We'll look at them separately, beginning with the issue of date.

The consistent teaching of the epistles is that the rapture is imminent, meaning that it could happen at any time with no events that must happen first. Paul speaks of the rapture as though he expected it in his lifetime. In 1 Thessalonians 4, writing about that event, he first explains that believers who have already died will return with Christ and receive their resurrection bodies. "Then we who are alive and remain will be caught up together with them in the clouds to meet the Lord in the air, and so we shall always be with the Lord" (v. 17). His use of the pronoun we suggests he expected to be in that group still alive on earth. This same dynamic can be seen in passages like 1 Corinthians 15:51, where Paul writes, "We shall not all sleep, but we shall all be changed." This certainly suggests he at least considered it possible that he would not experience physical death.

Interestingly, years later Paul seems to see the likelihood he will indeed die physically. In 2 Timothy he writes, "the time of my departure has come. I have fought the good fight, I have finished the race, I have kept the faith" (vv. 6-7). This gives us an example of the ideal way to live—as though Christ could return for us at any time but also ready to accept our death when God's appointed time comes.

Another important implication of this understanding of the time of the rapture is that all speculation that it will happen in the very near future, that current events and circumstances show it must be soon, has no biblical support. Since the rapture is imminent it might happen tomorrow afternoon, but because the Bible does not specify any necessary precursors it could just as easily be another millennium away.

The most common cause of this error—interpreting current events as an indication that the rapture must happen soon—is a misapplication of Christ's teachings in the Olivet Discourse (Matt. 24-25). In that teaching block Christ answers a question from the disciples on "the sign of your coming and of
the end of the age?" (Matt. 24:3). In the teaching that follows Christ talks about the coming of Messiah (24:5), the fulfillment of prophecy (24:15), an attack on Judea, observing the Sabbath (24:20), and a judgment of the nations
(25:32). These and other features indicate the Olivet Discourse taught the disciples about events that will precede Messiah's coming to establish Israel's promised kingdom on earth, not the rapture of the Body of Christ. Thus, the warnings about "wars and rumors of wars" (24:6) and "famines and earthquakes" (24:7) do not find their fulfillment in the circumstances of this age, but instead teach that prior to Messiah's return to Jerusalem to establish the kingdom these kinds of events will happen at an unprecedented level.

The rapture and Christ's coming to establish the kingdom promised to Israel have some features in common, which explains why they are often confused, with passages like the Olivet Discourse misunderstood as describing the rapture. In both cases we read of a trumpet (Matt. 24:31; 1 Thess. 4:16), the coming of the Lord (Matt. 25:31; 1 Thess. 4:16), and some taken while others remain (Matt. 24:40-44; 1 Thess. 4:17). But those similarities must be considered in the light of the significant differences that mark those two events as separate and distinct, one for the nation of Israel and one for the Body of Christ. Regarding the teaching that some are taken while others remain it's important to note that in Matthew 24:37-41 those who are taken are removed for judgment, whereas with the rapture those taken go to be with the Lord (1 Thess. 4:17-18).

Thus, we conclude that the rapture may take place at any moment and that no events are necessary precursors to Christ's coming to take away the portion of the Body of Christ still on earth. And this conclusion helps to answer the other question asked above: when does the rapture occur relative to other future events?

The rapture as an event separate and distinct from the second coming is one of the essential elements of dispensationalism. To be a dispensationalist means to believe in the rapture and to hold to Covenant theology means denying the rapture as a biblically predicted event distinct from the second coming. Covenant theology sees only one return of Christ, the one prophesied in the Old Testament and the Gospels.

In its classic form Covenant theology does not include a millennial reign of Christ on earth. According to this view passages that seem to teach about an earthly kingdom should better be interpreted allegorically and refer to the reign of Christ in the life of the believer. This view is known as a-millennialism, the prefix meaning no, or absence of. That is, there will be no thousand-year reign of Christ on earth.

For roughly the last 50-75 years the more common view within Covenant theology is that there will be a millennial reign of Christ on earth, but it will not favor Israel as God's special people. Christ will return at the second coming and set up a kingdom on earth, but it will be over all nations without distinction in the same way God's work is carried out today.

Because Covenant theology does not recognize different dispensations it has only this one eschatology in which Christ returns and establishes his rule on earth. It also does not believe in the tribulation as a literal seven-year period on earth. In Covenant theology the passages that seem to teach about it as a literal time period are instead about suffering and persecution in the believer's life.

Understanding these essential differences between the eschatology of Covenant theology and Dispensational theology will help us answer our second question, when the rapture occurs relative to other prophesied events. That is, it's a question unique to Dispensational theology because Covenant theology doesn't include a rapture.

The three options for the timing of the rapture are typically known as the pre-, mid-, and post-tribulation rapture positions and, as you probably guessed, they place the rapture in time relative to the tribulation. At the outset we note that if the rapture comes after any portion of the tribulation, either all of it or just the first half, then it is not truly imminent. This alone indicates the rapture precedes the tribulation, but many other key truths support that conclusion.

In his book, *Things to Come* (1958; Zondervan; Grand Rapids, MI), J. Dwight Pentecost gives 28 distinct biblical reasons why the rapture must happen before the tribulation. We won't repeat those here, but add just a few reasons from the perspective of mid-Acts dispensationalism.

- The tribulation is the subject of much Old Testament prophecy, including major sections in Daniel, Joel, and Ezekiel. It is an event on God's agenda for the nation Israel that serves a number of purposes, including purifying the nation for the arrival of their Messiah and the establishment of their promised kingdom. Zechariah 13:8-9 describes the terrible persecution Israel will suffer during the tribulation, with two thirds of the nation perishing and only one third preserved. "And I will put this third into the fire and refine them as one refines silver, and test them as gold is tested" (v. 9). The prophetic nature of the tribulation is inconsistent with the rapture as part of the mystery (1 Cor. 15:51-53).
- The tribulation is clearly a time of God's wrath poured out on the nations and on Israel as part of that refining process. Both the natural disasters and the persecutions of the Beast's reign make this period unprecedented. "If the Lord had not

cut short these days, no human being would be saved" (Mk. 13:20). Zephaniah 1 describes the day of the Lord (v. 1) as, "a day of distress and anguish, a day of ruin and devastation, a day of darkness and gloom, a day of clouds and thick darkness" (v. 15). This contrasts starkly with Paul's words of comfort to the Thessalonian church that, "God has not destined us for wrath, but to obtain salvation through our Lord Jesus Christ" (1 Thess. 5:9). To put the Body of Christ in any part of the tribulation certainly exposes us to God's wrath, not his salvation.

- Much of 2 Thessalonians is devoted to correcting a misunderstanding in the church caused by a false letter that claimed to be from Paul (see 2:1-2) telling them they were already in the tribulation, here referred to as the "day of the Lord." The believers in that city probably found it easy to believe this false teaching because of the persecution they had faced (see Acts 17:1-9; 1 Thess. 3:1-5), with the mention of those who have already died, perhaps referring to believers martyred for their faith (1 Thess. 4:13). In the second chapter of 2 Thessalonians Paul teaches them that the day of the Lord, the tribulation, cannot begin until the "man of lawlessness is revealed, the son of destruction who opposes and exalts himself against every so-called god or object of worship, so that he takes his seat in the temple of God, proclaiming himself to be God" (2 Thess. 2:3-4). Paul goes on to write that the anti-Christ is currently restrained, "so that he may be revealed in his time" (v. 6). "He who now restrains it will do so until he is out of the way. And then the lawless one will be revealed, whom the Lord Jesus will kill with the breath of his mouth and bring to nothing by the appearance of his coming" (vv. 7-8). There is some disagreement about the identity of the restrainer, but the most likely answer is the Holy Spirit, now present and working in the world primarily in and through members of the Body of Christ whom he indwells. If this is true, the Spirit's restraining work will continue until the Body of Christ is removed from the earth at the rapture. That event that will clear the way for the antichrist's emergence and the beginning of the tribulation.

- The position that the rapture takes place at the end of the tribulation is rare for good reason. Not only does it contradict Paul's teachings that God has not destined us for wrath (1 Thess. 5:9) but it creates an odd chronology. The second coming is the event that marks the end of the tribulation as Christ returns to rescue Israel at the eleventh hour from the onslaught of the beast (Rev. 19:19-21). A post-tribulation rapture requires that Christ come in the air for the Body of Christ, return to heaven, and then immediately come back to set up the kingdom. Why would those be separate yet adjacent events?

- Any view that the rapture takes place in the middle of the seven-year tribulation also has several overriding problems. The first is that it typically understands the first three and a half years as relatively peaceful and benign, with the persecutions beginning at the midway point. While it's clear conditions become extremely brutal and directed particularly at Israel when Satan is cast to earth at that halfway point (Dan. 9:27; Rev. 12:7-17), it would be incorrect to infer the first half of the tribulation isn't a also a time of wrath and persecution. The opening section of the Olivet Discourse describes a time of wars, rumors of wars, famines, and earthquakes in various places. "All these are the beginnings of birth pains" (Matt. 24:4-8). Christ continues, "Then you will be handed over to be persecuted and put to death and you will be hated by all nations because of me" (v. 9). This change from the beginning of birth pains with natural calamities and international conflicts to intense persecution focused on Israel seems to correspond to the midpoint of the tribulation when Satan is cast to earth. Thus, while there is a change in the focus and intensity of persecution at the midpoint of the tribulation the entire seven years is a time of God's wrath. And again, the entire seven years of the tribulation is the subject of prophecy and therefore inconsistent with the dispensation of Grace, which was a secret. The eschatology of the Body of Christ is described by Paul as a mystery (1 Cor. 15:51).

After questions about the timing of the rapture it's natural to wonder about the way in which it will occur. The believers in Corinth were understandably curious about the kind of bodies they would have after the resurrection, and Paul answered that question in 1 Corinthians 15:35-49. He says our resurrection bodies will be completely different from our earthly bodies and will be imperishable, incorruptible, and like Christ's resurrection body, bearing "the image of the man of heaven" (v. 49). This fits with what John wrote, that, "when he appears we shall be like him, because we shall see him as he is" (1 Jn. 3:2). The New Testament presents Christ's resurrection body as the prototype of the believer's resurrection body (see 1 Cor. 15:22-23).

We don't know a lot about Christ's resurrection body, only able to infer characteristics from the post-resurrection narratives in the Gospels and Acts. But from those passages we know his body was physical because the disciples were able to touch it (Lk. 24:39). Interestingly, he ate food with the disciples (Lk. 24:41-43), though eating was not necessary because his glorified body was incorruptible and imperishable. Rather, it was a way of showing the disciples he did indeed have a body and was not just a ghost or apparition.

It's harder to know what to do with the presence of the marks of crucifixion still present on Christ's resurrection body (Jn. 20:27). When considered in light of Paul's teachings about the glorified nature of the resurrection body it seems likely that Christ's body bore these marks to assure the disciples that he was indeed the same one they saw crucified three days earlier, an exception to the norm in order to undeniably establish this important fact.

One question the Bible doesn't address is the way in which believers on earth will receive their resurrection bodies at the instant of the rapture. Most of us have wondered if the bodies of Christians will mysteriously and visibly ascend into the clouds to be transformed or if believers' bodies will fall limp and lifeless wherever they are at that moment with their spirits ascending to a point in the firmament where new bodies will be received. Either of those two options would seem likely to create a worldwide panic that would throw the population of the world into chaos. Does this terror set the stage for those who remain to accept the reign of the antichrist?

The Bible is silent on the matter, so this is one of those questions about which we can only speculate. But it seems significant that everywhere the New Testament speaks to the nature of our present physical bodies it speaks of them in disparaging terms. Paul says, "For I know that nothing good dwells in me, that is, in my flesh" (Rom. 7:18). And in the section of 1 Corinthians 15 where he discusses the resurrection body (vv. 35-49) Paul makes it clear our present physical bodies are not fit for eternity and cannot compare to what we will receive. This seems to make it more likely that our new glorified bodies will be created "from scratch," not in a mid-air transformation of our present bodies thoroughly corrupted by sin. This would parallel the creation of the new heaven and the new earth, which God brings into being after the destruction of the present creation (Rev. 21:1).

Our earthly bodies are a stewardship from God, temples of the Holy Spirit (1 Cor. 6:19-20), our unique characteristics an expression of God's good and sovereign will. But the effects of sin on the flesh are so thorough and the glory of our future bodies so radical that the two seem incompatible.

Of course the third option is, "none of the above." God is certainly capable of creating circumstances that would result in the disappearance of millions of bodies with a readily believed explanation. For example, that could happen through a man-made event or a natural disaster.

In 2 Thessalonians 2:9-10 Paul writes that the coming of the lawless one "is by the activity of Satan with all power and false signs and wonders, and with all wicked deception for those who are perishing, because they refused to love the truth and so be saved." He adds that "God sends them a strong delusion, so that they may believe what is false" (v. 11). Paul doesn't specify what that strong delusion is, but the lie may be an explanation for the disappearance of millions that causes humanity to accept an explanation other than the rapture of the saints.

Another matter on which the Bible is silent is the time span between the rapture and the beginning of the tribulation. The latter requires, as we've already noted from 2 Thessalonians 2:3-4, the appearance of the antichrist. Many of us have assumed these two events, the rapture and the beginning of the tribulation, happen in fairly quick succession. But there may be good reason to think they are separated by a significant span of time, perhaps a full generation or more.

Throughout history the dispensational changes have each been marked by a judgment (see Understanding Your Bible). Nowhere does Scripture say each dispensation must end with a great judgment, but that has certainly been the pattern, including expulsion from the garden, the worldwide flood, the confusion of languages, the Egyptian slavery, and the setting aside of Israel. In Understanding Your Bible we identified the failure for the dispensation of Grace to be the rejection by the vast majority of Jesus Christ's atoning work. That leads us to ask, what might be the judgment for the dispensation of Grace?

One possibility is that the tribulation serves as the judgment. It certainly qualifies as terrible, and it effects the whole world, a fitting parallel to the test of the dispensation of Grace in which all of mankind is called to respond to the gospel. Some have noted, however, that early in the seven-year period the judgments on the earth are delayed until 144,000 servants of God are sealed and protected from harm (Rev. 7:1-

8). These servants, taken from the tribes of Israel, go out to evangelize the earth. John then saw "a great multitude that no one could number, from every nation, from all the tribes and peoples and languages, standing before the throne and before the Lamb, clothed in white robes, with palm branches in their hands" (v. 9). John asks who these people wearing white robes are and is told, "These are the ones coming out of the great tribulation. They have washed their robes and made them white in the blood of the Lamb" (v. 14).

God had three great purposes for raising up the nation of Israel. He decreed they would be the channel through which the Savior of the world would come, he chose them to be the repository, the storehouse for his Word, and he ordained them to be the instrument for evangelizing the world. The nations hearing the gospel is not the mystery revealed to Paul, but rather that they now receive it on equal footing with Israel, with no distinction (Eph. 3:4-6; Gal. 3:28). God's intent that Israel be his means of spreading the gospel explains what is called the Great Commission (Matt. 28:19) and his prediction to the apostles that they would be his witnesses "to the end of the earth" (Acts 1:8).

We note that Israel fulfilled the first two purposes God had in choosing them. The Savior did indeed come as the descendant of the Jewish patriarchs, and all of Scripture up until this dispensation was given to and preserved by Israel. However, rather than become God's instrument for taking the gospel to the world they rejected the Savior and as a result were set aside.

Revelation 7 teaches us that the purposes of God will not be frustrated, and that in the tribulation 144,000 witnesses drawn from the tribes of Israel and protected from harm by God will spread the gospel throughout the world, with an innumerable multitude saved. This will fulfill the prophesy of Zechariah: "In those days ten men from the nations of every tongue shall take hold of the robe of a Jew, saying, 'Let us go with you, for we have heard that God is with you'" (Zech. 8:23).

This and the distinctively Jewish nature of the tribulation have led some Bible students to ask if the seven-year period makes a fitting judgment for the dispensation of Grace. People who had rejected the gospel prior to the rapture could accept it through the ministry of the 144,000 if the tribulation begins immediately after the rapture. This leads to the suggestion that a generation or more will pass between the rapture and the tribulation, a generation left without any witness to the gospel, thus leaving them without the means for hearing and receiving it (see Rom. 10:14). It also explains why the 144,000 must be raised up by God through his direct action, since there are no believers on earth to tell them of the gospel. Their salvation would be similar to Paul's conversion on the road to Damascus.

The details of specifically when and where believers on earth will get their new bodies and the amount of time between the rapture and the tribulation are examples of the uncertainty we referred to earlier. We can only speculate based on the limited information the Bible gives us and what seems reasonable. They are worthwhile questions to the extent they take us to the Word, and should be set aside if they lead to quarrels and controversies (2 Tim. 2:23). What is certain is that our Sovereign God will work out all the details according to his perfect will and may surprise us in the process.

IMPLICATIONS AND APPLICATIONS

During the last decades of the 1800s and the early part of the 1900s the Bible-conference movement spread rapidly across the U.S., with eschatology becoming a major theme. These prophecy conferences and the Scofield Reference Bible, which first appeared in 1909, contributed to the spread of dispensationalism and the understanding that the rapture and the second coming are separate events. Eschatology became a major part of the preaching and teaching of the time, often with a sharp and harsh division between groups with a Covenant and Dispensational perspective.

Over the last several decades the contemporary church has lost its interest in eschatology and it's rare to hear a sermon or lesson that takes up the kind of topics discussed in this section. Identifying the reasons for this shift makes for an interesting study in cultural dynamics, but there can be no question that the church and individual believers miss out if the Bible's teaching on the future is ignored.

We began this section by noting that the Bible doesn't give us as much detail about the future as most of us would like. But the significant amount we are told indicates God wants his people to know key truths about the future. This information, like all biblical truth, can and should have an effect on life. Thus, the decline in interest among Christians in biblical eschatology brings with it an associated weakness in the spiritual health of believers and their churches.

We naturally tend to focus on what's in front of us, on the events, problems, and challenges of the moment. The biblical record reminds us that God is working his great plan, which began in the garden and will proceed through to eternity. By his sovereignty the rise and fall of world empires have happened at the precise times and in the specific ways God directed. His sovereign will also extends to what seem at first glance to be the most insignificant events, like a mother's decision to hide her son in a basket among the reeds in the Nile River or a new king choosing what was then a small town to be his nation's capital.

God's promises about the future are sure and certain, a confidence we have in part based on seeing his work through history. And just as events large and small were directed in order that they led to the cross and our salvation, so events large and small will be directed in order that they will lead to our eternal presence in his glorious kingdom (2 Tim. 4:18). The Bible's teaching about the future, when combined with the record of God's work through history, assures us God has a plan, he is in control of all things in order that his plan will come to pass, and the end will be glorious for all who by faith have accepted his gracious provision of salvation.

This should result in a number of responses from God's people. Any tendency to panic or despair at current events must be outweighed by the assurance that "God works all things together for good" for those who are called according to his purpose (Rom. 8:28). We must take the long view, less consumed by our immediate circumstances and more focused on God's great plan for history. This far-sightedness is modeled by the patriarchs who, when faced with sometimes desperate circumstances, looked for a city "whose designer and maker is God" (Heb. 11:10). As the song says, "This world is not my home, I'm just a-passing through."

This confidence should also bring peace when we face physical death. Most of us will die from disease, not a fatal accident, so we'll likely see death coming. When Paul got to that point he wrote to Timothy with calm confidence about the future awaiting him. His words in 2 Timothy 4:6-8 were penned while in a Roman jail cell, knowing his execution was near. Yet there is no hint of fear, hesitation, or withdrawal.

Trials have a way of bringing our core convictions to the surface, including our beliefs about the future. This is powerfully illustrated in the songs of the slaves now known as spirituals. Under cruel conditions with words that drew heavily from biblical stories they sang of crossing the Jordan, chariots coming to carry them home, receiving a robe and a crown, and arriving on Canaan's shore. Contemporary believers, after decades of ignoring the Bible's teachings on our promised eternal deliverance, are not well equipped to endure even modest trials and far too inclined to self-pity.

But the most important outcome of studying what Scripture teaches about the future should be the humble worship it produces. Our great God is not only sovereign over all of history, over events large and small, he is also gracious to those who by faith turn to him for salvation. The Body of Christ will have no part in the tribulation. If any of us remains alive on earth when he comes for the Body we will, in an instant, receive our glorified bodies. We may not know the way that will happen, but it will happen. God's Word is sure and certain. In a world that can look so random and chaotic we praise our Father who has secured our eternal destiny in his presence.

Questions

1. What explanation would you give for the declining interest in what the Bible teaches about future events?
2. Can you identify specific contrasts between Christ's return described in Matthew 24 and the rapture described in 1 Thessalonians 4:13-18?
3. Identify two passages that teach the rapture is imminent.
4. Identify biblical reasons for concluding the rapture will precede the tribulation.
5. What impact on the daily life of the believer should the imminency of the rapture have?

WHAT ABOUT THE BODY OF CHRIST AFTER THE RAPTURE?

The reign of Christ on earth is very Jewish in many of its characteristics. It thus became common among mid-Acts dispensationalists to understand that reign as uniquely for Israel and not involving the Body of Christ in any sense. Israel looks for the return and reign of Messiah from Jerusalem (Zech. 14:8-11) while we wait for the coming of Christ to meet the Lord in the air (1 Thess. 4:16-17). This difference leads many to conclude that the complete distinction between our two hopes is central to mid-Acts dispensationalism. However, Paul uses the word kingdom in many of his letters, requiring us to look more closely at what the Bible says on the subject.

Perhaps the best place to start resolving the question of our role in the kingdom is by looking at the relevant section in Revelation without any presuppositions regarding the kingdom's participants.

The end of Revelation describes the defeat of the beast and the false prophet, who will rule earth during the tribulation and of the armies gathered with them to wage war against Christ. The armies will be killed with the sword coming out of the mouth of the rider on the horse (the command of Christ) and the beast and false prophet thrown alive into the lake of burning sulfur (19:20). The opening section of chapter 21 tells us that Satan is then bound for a thousand years in the Abyss (20:2), which begins the time we call the millennial kingdom.

The result of this victory by Christ is that the earth has a population made up of those who lived through the tribulation but had not joined the army to wage war against Christ. That is, these are people in their natural bodies who survived the tribulation and enter the millennial kingdom where Christ rules.

In 20:4-5 we read that those who were martyred for their faith during the tribulation are resurrected and reign with Christ for a thousand years, an event called "the first resurrection." The result is that the residents of earth during the millennial kingdom are both people in their natural bodies and resurrected saints martyred during the tribulation. While a mix of pre- and post-resurrection individuals living side by side might seem strange, it parallels the presence of Christ among the disciples following his resurrection. This millennial situation is not unprecedented.

From the text of Revelation we might assume this group—those who survived the tribulation and the battle at Christ's return and those martyred during the tribulation now given their resurrection bodies—are the only participants in the kingdom. However, in Matthew 19:28 Christ said to the Twelve, "Truly I tell you, at the renewal of all things, when the Son of Man sits on his glorious throne, you who have followed me will also sit on twelve thrones, judging the twelve tribes of Israel." This indicates the disciples will be part of the first resurrection (Rev. 20:5) and present on earth during this kingdom.

This leads us to ask if other believers from the dispensations of Promise and/or Law will be resurrected for the millennial kingdom. When Christ told the Twelve they would rule, did they understand that to mean they would rule over their contemporaries who would also be there? That certainly seems likely because they expected the kingdom to be established at any moment. The crucifixion was not part of their thinking, and on the Mount of Olives just before the ascension they asked Christ if he would establish the kingdom at that point. Because the dispensation of Grace was a secret they had no idea there would be a delay of more than 2,000 years before Messiah would return to establish his rule in Jerusalem. Thus, because the Twelve expected the kingdom to begin soon they would have understood Christ's promise to them regarding their rule to include the presence of their contemporaries as the subjects of that rule.

If the Twelve and their believing contemporaries will be resurrected and present at the millennial kingdom many have concluded that all believers from the dispensations of Promise and Law, or at least from Law, will also be resurrected and present. Many passages in the Prophets speak of the reign of Messiah and describe it as the hope of Israel, the blessing that follows suffering. Though there's no specific statement about this in Revelation 21 it seems reasonable to conclude the first resurrection will include all the redeemed from Israel's history. God is faithful to keep his promises, which are irrevocable (Rom. 11:29). The text in Revelation focuses on the circumstances of that point in time, meaning that the absence of any mention of Old Testament saints as participants in the first resurrection cannot be taken to mean they won't be included.

Here then is another example of some ambiguity in Scripture on one of the details of eschatology that reminds us dogmatism regarding specifics is unwarranted. But if we are correct that those present in the millennial kingdom will include survivors from the tribulation and resurrected saints from the Old Testament and martyrs from the tribulation we likely have a situation in which resurrected individuals outnumber those in their natural bodies.

At this point we can ask what, if any, role members of the Body of Christ will have in the kingdom. In 1 Thessalonians 4:17 Paul says that as a result of the rapture members of the Body of Christ, "will always be with the Lord." Many passages make clear that during the millennial kingdom Christ will reign physically on earth from Jerusalem (see Isa. 2:2-4; Zech. 14:16-17). Because the rapture precedes the kingdom, during which Christ will reign over the earth from Jerusalem, and because we will always be with Christ, it seems reasonable to conclude we will also be on earth during his millennial reign. Like those listed above, we will be in our resurrection bodies.

One might respond that as a member of the Trinity Christ is omnipresent, which means we would be with him during the kingdom even though he would be on earth and we would be in heaven. But that makes Paul's statement in 1 Thessalonians 4 meaningless. In that passage he writes that as a result of meeting Christ in the air earthly members of the Body of Christ will, from that point onward, always be with him. If the omnipresence of Christ means that during the millennial kingdom we are present with Christ despite being in heaven while he is on earth, it must also mean that we are present with Christ now and that no real change occurs at the rapture. What, then, is the point of Paul's teaching in 1 Thessalonians 4? Why would he write that as a result of the rapture, "we will always be with the Lord" (1 Thess. 4:17)?

In the section on the Gospels we noted that the Bible uses the word kingdom in what seems to be five different ways:

- God's *universal kingdom*, which encompasses all things and is the result of his sovereignty (Ps. 22:28).
- The *political kingdoms*, the earthly governments that come and go throughout history (Deut. 3:21).
- God's *spiritual kingdom,* which contains all the redeemed who are God's subjects, under his care and will (Col. 1:13).
- The *millennial kingdom* promised to Israel, when Messiah will rule from Jerusalem (Micah 4:3-8).
- The *eschatological kingdom,* which is future, eternal, and composed only of believers (1 Cor. 6:9-11).

It could be said that the spiritual kingdom and the eschatological kingdom are essentially the same, the former existing within time and the latter consisting of the same group (all the redeemed) in eternity. The difference between the two kingdoms would be the dynamics of the relationship between God and the subjects of the kingdom who are affected by the presence (within time) or absence (in eternity) of a sinful environment.

Paul uses the word kingdom 14 times in eight of his letters. In order to decide if he gives instruction on our participation in the millennial kingdom we need to look at each of those 14 passages and determine which kingdom Paul refers to.

Paul never seems to use the word *kingdom* to refer to God's universal kingdom or the political kingdoms of earth. That is not to say he doesn't recognize them, just that he doesn't use the word *kingdom* when discussing them.

He clearly uses *kingdom* to refer to the spiritual realm in which God exercises authority and care over believers on earth. For example, he tells the believers in Rome that, "The kingdom of God is not a matter of eating and drinking, but of righteousness and peace and joy in the holy Spirit" (Rom. 14:17). This same description of the life of a child of God seems to be in his mind in 1 Corinthians 4:20, Colossians 1:13, and 4:11, placing the kingdom in the context of this present time. The word kingdom in 1 Thessalonians 2:12 could refer to the life of a believer in this present age or to an eschatological kingdom. Paul writes, "walk in a manner worthy of God, who calls you into his own kingdom and glory."

The future eternal kingdom over which Christ rules after the end of time and of this creation seems clearly in Paul's mind in some of the other passages where he uses that word, especially where the verbs are in the future tense and the context describes the final state. For example, in 1 Corinthians 6:9-10 he writes that the unrighteous will not inherit the kingdom of God. In 1 Corinthians 15:50 Paul writes that "flesh and blood cannot inherit the kingdom of God," yet we know that the millennial kingdom will include people still in their earthly bodies who survive the tribulation.

There are at most six places where Paul uses the word *kingdom* and may be referring to the millennial kingdom, where Christ rules from Jerusalem for a thousand years. However, each of these can also be understood to refer to one of the other kingdoms.

- 1 Corinthians 1:9, "Or do you not know that the unrighteous will not inherit the kingdom of God?" And in v. 10, "...nor swindlers will inherit the kingdom of God." The most natural reading of these two verses is a reference to a future kingdom and has them referring to the eternal kingdom. They could conceivably refer to the millennial kingdom if they refer to those resurrected at the first resurrection (Rev. 20:1-5). That is, unrepentant and unregenerate sinners will not be resurrected to participate in the millennial kingdom. But that seems like an unnecessary point for Paul to make and inconsistent with the context of this section of 1 Corinthians.

- 1 Corinthians 15:24, "Then comes the end, when he delivers the kingdom to God the Father after destroying every rule and every authority and power." This interesting verse focuses on an event involving a kingdom, not the kingdom itself. Paul describes a point in time when Christ will deliver the kingdom to the Father and specifies this will happen after Christ has destroyed all inferior rulers and kingdoms. In the prior verse he mentions an event that will precede this destruction of all competing kingdoms, namely the resurrections of "Christ the firstfruits, then at his coming those who belong to Christ" (v. 23). This seems to group both the rapture and the first resurrection together inasmuch as those individuals both fit the description, "those who belong to Christ," that is, are redeemed. Thus, after the resurrection of Christ and the resurrection of all the redeemed he destroys all inferior kingdoms, and then delivers the kingdom to the Father. To which kingdom does Paul refer? Of the five we've identified the most likely seems to be Christ's universal kingdom. As the next several verses indicate, that universal kingdom, which embodies God's sovereign control over all things, is now ruled by the Son because, "God has put all things in subjection under his feet" (v. 27). But at what is sometimes called the *consummation*, the Son will present this kingdom to the Father as an act of submission so that "the Son himself will also be subjected to him who put all things in subjection under him, that God may be all in all" (v. 28).

- 2 Thessalonians 1.5, "This is evidence of the righteous judgment of God, that you may be considered worthy of the kingdom of God, for which you are also suffering." The kingdom Paul has in mind here seems to be in the future with its blessings that God will give to those who have suffered for their faith. That it is future means this kingdom is either the millennial kingdom or the eternal kingdom that begins after the great white throne judgment when the eternal destiny of both the saved and unsaved is determined. The latter is what Paul intends, something made clear in the next few verses. He says when Christ is revealed those who do not know God "will suffer the punishment of eternal destruction, away from the presence of the Lord and from the glory of his might" (v. 9). That is, the eternal judgment of those who do not know God coincides with the blessings of the kingdom given to the saints.

- 2 Timothy 4:1-2, "I charge you in the presence of God and of Christ Jesus, who is to judge the living and the dead, and by his appearing and his kingdom: preach the word; be ready in season and out of season; reprove, rebuke, and exhort, with complete patience and teaching." Again, the reference to the coming judgment makes it clear Paul has one of the two future kingdoms in mind. That judgment could be associated with Christ's second coming and the battle of Armageddon that precedes the millennial kingdom (Rev. 19:11-21) or with the battle of Gog and Magog, which is followed by the Great White Throne and the eternal kingdom (Rev. 20:7-15). Since he doesn't elaborate it's probably not possible to say with certainty which of those two kingdoms he has in mind. But perhaps the solemn charge to Timothy fits best with the eternal kingdom and the final resolution and restoration of all things.

- 2 Timothy 4:18, "The Lord will rescue me from every evil deed and bring me safely into his heavenly kingdom. To him be the glory forever and ever. Amen." This reference to the kingdom also looks to the future and Paul's assurance that, even as he nears the end of his life and faces martyrdom, he will see God's heavenly kingdom. Here, too, we lack enough information in the form of context or content to make a definitive decision regarding which of the two future kingdoms Paul has in mind, the millennial kingdom or the eternal kingdom. However, the fact Paul describes this as a heavenly kingdom may suggest he has the eternal kingdom in mind.

After this look at Paul's use of the word *kingdom* we are left about where we started. We have no clear statement in Paul's letters that we will be present in the millennial kingdom, but in 1 Thessalonians 4:17 he tells us that after the rapture "we will always be with the Lord." During the Millennium Christ will rule from Jerusalem. Therefore, our presence on earth with him during that time seems to be the only reasonable conclusion. Paul spends little, if any time writing about it, indicating the millennial kingdom is not the focus of our future. Instead, the eternal kingdom was Paul's ultimate hope.

If Paul's long-term focus was the eternal kingdom, the next step is to ask about the eternal state of the Body of Christ relative to Israel. Do dispensational distinctions continue in eternity or are the redeemed of all dispensations together in God's presence?

This question probably gets too little attention and may be an example of jumping to what look like good answers without the kind of careful examination of the Scripture that brought commendation to the Bereans (Acts 17:11). We'll begin our exploration of this topic by again noting that on some issues the Bible is not explicit, and on those matters we should be careful not to draw lines of division. Our discussion of a question like dispensational distinctions in eternity must happen in the context of eager and collegial Bible study, not with a view to defining a standard of orthodoxy that doesn't stand up to Scripture.

It has been typical for mid-Acts dispensationalists to understand the Body of Christ as completely separate and distinct from Israel both in this life and the life to come, including our eternal destinies. Passages understood to support this view include Philippians 4:20 where Paul writes that, "our citizenship is in heaven." This contrasts with Israel's promise of an eternal kingdom on earth (see Isa. 9:6-7). We are seated "with him in the heavenly places" (Eph. 2:6), we have a house "eternal in the heavens" (2 Cor. 5:1), and Paul looked forward to being brought "safely into his heavenly kingdom" (2 Tim. 4:18). These passages contrast with those addressed to Israel that focus on their hope for a kingdom on earth ruled by their Messiah, leading many mid-Acts dispensationalists to conclude the distinctions between Israel and the Body of Christ continue into eternity, with our location and destinies separate in the life to come.

One of the associated affirmations of this view is that the Bride of Christ is Israel, and any identification of the Body of Christ as the Bride seriously confuses God's two programs. This, it is maintained, is clear just from the terms used, since Christ cannot marry his own body.

In Revelation 21 and 22, which describes events after the millennial kingdom, the New Jerusalem which descends from heaven after the great white throne judgment, is said to be the Bride of Christ (Rev. 21:2, 9-10). The New Jerusalem is clearly used metaphorically here because a Person cannot marry a city. However, the description of the city in Revelation 21 certainly evokes images of the nation of Israel with the mention of 12 gates adorned with 12 pearls each and its size (12,000 stadia square). In Isaiah 62:4-5 the prophet says to Zion: "You shall no more be termed Forsaken and your land shall no more be termed Desolate, but you shall be called My Delight Is in Her, and your land Married; For the Lord delights in you, and your land shall be married." These passages associate Israel with the imagery of the bride wedded to their Messiah.

However, several questions present themselves when we take the view that dispensational distinctions will continue in eternity and that Israel is the Bride of Christ in Revelation 21 and 22. For example, what happens to believers from the dispensations before God began his program with Israel? Whether we identify that point as God's calling of Abraham or the giving of Israel's constitution at Sinai, there are thousands of years and an unknown number of generations of redeemed individuals who, under this scenario, have an unspecified eternal destiny. Their eternal life is secure in God, but they were neither members of the nation of Israel or the Body of Christ. Is there some third location for them to dwell through eternity?

In the chapter on salvation in *Understanding Your Bible* we noted that the matter of salvation is not associated with dispensations but wholly dependent on the individual's acceptance or rejection of God's provision of atonement, whether through an animal sacrifice made through faith or through the acceptance of Christ's atoning work on the cross. Thus, the faith of the individual, regardless of the dispensation in which they lived, is what determines their eternal destiny. All the redeemed before the cross were saved because by faith they believed that God accepted their animal sacrifice as payment for their sins. All those after the cross are saved because they believe that Christ paid the full price for their sins when he gave his life for them. This alone strongly suggests that dispensational distinctions are irrelevant in eternity and that the exercise of saving faith is the unifying element for all the redeemed throughout history. Why, then, would dispensational distinctions continue?

Further evidence that the distinctions between Israel and the Body of Christ are not rigid and do not extend into eternity appears in Romans. Paul tells us that God set Israel aside because of their unbelief (Rom. 11:20), and the record in early Acts reflects that. When presented with the message that Jesus was their Messiah and that repentance would bring about his return to establish their promised kingdom, Israel rejected both the message and the messengers. They persecuted and jailed the apostles and stoned Stephen. Paul says the branches of Israel were broken off because of their unbelief (Rom 11:20) and the Gentiles were "grafted in among the others and now share in the nourishing root of the olive tree" (v. 17). In anticipation of what will happen in the future he adds, "And even they, if they do not continue in their unbelief, will be grafted in, for God has the power to graft them in again" (v. 23). This description of the dispensational relationships using the grafting analogy strongly suggests a core connection between Israel and the Body of Christ, specifically the response of faith to the goodness and blessings of God. Faith is the single essential element in a relationship with God regardless of the dispensation. As Hebrews 11 makes clear by examples from throughout biblical history, "Without faith it is impossible to please him, for whoever would draw near to God must believe that he exists and that he rewards those who seek him" (v. 6). It's hard to see why Paul would use the analogy of grafting onto a common root if the distinctions between Israel and the Body of Christ were total and permanent. Instead, it is the presence or absence of faith that is determinative.

In Revelation 21:3, in connection with the descent of the New Jerusalem, we read: "And I heard a loud voice from the throne saying, 'Behold, the dwelling place of God is with man. He will dwell with them, and they will be his people, and God himself will be with them as their God.'" In 1 Thessalonians 4:17, describing the rapture, Paul says: "Then we who are alive, who are left, will be caught up together with them in the clouds to meet the Lord in the air, and so we will always be with the Lord." How can it be that the eternal location of the Body of Christ is in heaven with the Lord and he is also eternally present in the New Jerusalem on earth?

If God will be present in the New Jerusalem and if "we will always be with the Lord," it's appropriate to reconsider the nature of the New Jerusalem and the identity of the Bride of Christ. In this context a verse from one of Paul's letters stands out as especially noteworthy.

In Galatians 4 Paul argues against the Jewish legalism that had taken hold in the churches of that region. In the second half of the chapter he draws an analogy, writing that, "Hagar is Mount Sinai in Arabia; she corresponds to the present Jerusalem, for she is in slavery with her children" (v. 25). That is, Hagar was a slave woman (v. 22) and her son Ishmael was born according to the flesh (v. 23). Paul uses the slave Hagar and her son, born outside the promise of God, as analogous to the Law given at Mount Sinai and corresponding to the present, earthly Jerusalem. Those who submit to the Law are the descendants of Hagar and Ishmael, slaves to the Law as represented by the present Jerusalem.

By contrast, Sarah and her son, Isaac, were free, and Isaac the son of promise (v. 23). Just as Abraham was told to cast out the slave woman and her son (v. 30), so the Galatian believers should cast out the legalism of adherence to the Law because, "we are not children of the slave, but of the free woman" (v. 31).

Paul contrasts Sarah the free woman and her son born according to the promise with Hagar, who corresponds to the present Jerusalem, which is in slavery. "But the Jerusalem above is free, and she is our mother" (v. 26). The most natural understanding of Paul's words, "the Jerusalem above" is what is called the New Jerusalem in Revelation, a city that descends from heaven. "And she is our mother."

In Hebrews 8 we read about a temple in heaven that served as a pattern for the tabernacle Moses built in the wilderness. What Moses built was, "a copy and shadow of the heavenly things" (v. 5). In chapter 9 it says, "through the greater and more perfect tent (not made with hands, that is, not of this creation) he entered once for all into the holy places, not by means of the blood of goats and calves, but by means of his own blood, thus securing an eternal redemption" (v. 12). Christ has entered "once for all into the holy places, not into holy places made with hands, which are copies of the true things, but into heaven itself, now to appear in the presence of God on our behalf" (v. 24).

There is in heaven the true Tabernacle of which Moses' version was but a humble shadow. It was into this heavenly Tabernacle that Christ entered, offering up his own blood as payment for our sins. All who accept that work of Christ on their behalf are the beneficiaries of the gracious gift that secured our atonement and eternal life. This is true regardless of our dispensational position within this present creation.

The heavenly temple, which had an earthly shadow version with Israel, is the site of the great transaction that secured our atonement regardless of our dispensational position. So also the New Jerusalem is "our mother" and the eternal center for all the redeemed from all of human history. The earthly tabernacle certainly had a connection with the nation of Israel, as does the earthly Jerusalem, but neither of these precludes both the heavenly temple and the heavenly Jerusalem from having a greater role for all believers throughout the dispensations.

How, then, should we understand the very Jewish characteristics of the New Jerusalem with a description that includes so many references to the number 12? Can the eternal city be both Jewish in its characteristics and universal with regard to its inhabitants? If dispensational distinctions do not continue into eternity and all believers from all of history dwell together, why would it be in a place with features so connected to Israel?

Prior to Genesis 12 and the calling of Abraham we have no indication that God was going to carry out his gracious plan for mankind through a specific individual and his offspring. Through the rest of Genesis we learn that God's plan narrowed further from Abraham to Jacob and his sons. God changed Jacob's name to Israel (Gen. 32:28) and his descendants, the Israelites, became God's special nation at Mt. Sinai (Ex. 19:5-6). From that point until the revelation of the mystery to the apostle Paul the Jews held that position of privilege before God. Now, in the dispensation of Grace, there is no distinction between Jew and Gentile and no special position for the descendants of Jacob (Gal. 3:28; Eph. 3:6; Col. 3:11).

As often as Paul writes about the equality of Jew and Gentile in this dispensation (the three passages in the previous sentence are a small sample), his words and actions in other places seem odd. For example, in Romans 9:1-5 he lists the many benefits that came to that nation because of their selection by a sovereign God, benefits he expresses in the present tense.

It was Paul's habit, when entering a new city, to go first to the synagogue and only move to the marketplace after he had preached the gospel and been rejected by that Jewish audience. The most common explanation for this pattern is that he knew the synagogue presented hearers who were monotheistic and who accepted the authority of what we call the Old Testament. Thus, the synagogue seemed to present the most sympathetic audience. But as we know, and as Paul certainly would have either known from the beginning or figured out quickly, those Jews in the synagogue were especially hostile to his message.

So instead of a purely pragmatic reason for starting in the synagogue Paul may have understood that Israel continued to hold a special place in God's plan. That is, the nation of Israel holds no place of *preference* over the Gentiles but still holds a place of special *honor*. Paul writes, "As regards the gospel, they are enemies for your sake. But as regards election, they are beloved for the sake of their forefathers. For the gifts and the calling of God are irrevocable" (Rom. 11:28-29).

God graciously and sovereignly chose Israel as the means through which he would bring salvation to the world. One step in that process, their carrying the message of salvation to the world as expressed in what's called the Great Commission, failed because they refused to accept Jesus as the promised Messiah, who brought that salvation. As a result, God in his abounding grace set the nation aside and presented the gospel to Jew and Gentile alike without distinction. We read in the Bible that at some point in the future God will resume his dealings with

Israel, bringing them to repentance and fulfilling all his promises to them.

It seems to best fit the totality of the biblical narrative to understand that God's love for Israel continues through this dispensation even when their favored position is temporarily set aside. In the Old Testament Israel had the blessing of the tabernacle in their midst, a shadow of the eternal heavenly place where redemption was accomplished. After God carries out his final judgment and restores creation to his perfect design, the eternal city, our mother (Gal. 4:26), will become the dwelling place for all the redeemed of history. We will live together, forever in his presence. Just as the earthly tabernacle given to Israel was just a pattern of the reality in heaven, so their earthly Jerusalem was but a pattern of the heavenly city that will descend.

Thus, we distinguish between honor and privilege. If our analysis is correct Israel has been temporarily set aside in terms of their position of privilege relative to the Gentiles, but their place of love and honor in God's sight continues and will continue into eternity. Israel was given the tabernacle, a shadow of the heavenly reality that in its form showed its connection with the nation (for example, the 12 loaves on the table of showbread). The New Jerusalem likewise reflects God's sovereign love for the nation. Just as we are beneficiaries of the transaction carried out in the heavenly tabernacle, so we will be residents of the heavenly city.

IMPLICATIONS AND APPLICATIONS

In their early stages groups tend to define and describe themselves by their differences from others. A new business might say, "We're not like the other guys. We provide same-day service." A social action group says, "We want to address this pressing need in society that has gone largely ignored." And a newly formed religious body identifies itself by the doctrines or commitments that set it apart from other organizations. This dynamic is both understandable and effective in explaining the new group's reason for forming and for drawing in others who share the same core commitments.

A problem can develop if the organization begins to overstate or over-emphasize the things that make it distinctive. This tendency is also understandable, especially when there is opposition from those outside that leads members to a defensive presentation of their distinctives. If differences become the primary way a group bonds together, the overstatement of those distinctions often follows.

When what became the Grace Gospel Fellowship took shape in the early 1940s the men who began that association often came under scathing criticism from other Bible teachers and denominations. Their courageous commitment to mid-Acts dispensationalism became a major theme in their preaching, teaching, and writings, with an emphasis on the uniqueness of Paul's ministry. Did that emphasis sometimes lead to overstating distinctions between Paul's teaching and that of other biblical authors? Have some within mid-Acts dispensationalism seen differences in the writings of biblical authors where none exists? If so, it would be an understandable if unfortunate response with many parallels both inside and outside the theological arena.

Our look at the participation of members of the Body of Christ in the millennial kingdom suggests that may have happened in some cases. Other examples of this dynamic include the matter of miracles within this dispensation. Some mid-Acts dispensationalists have wrongly concluded that God is not doing miracles in this dispensation, an error that comes from failing to distinguish between direct and indirect miracles and the purposes for each class (see Understanding Your Bible).

The tendency to overstate distinctions may come from a variety of causes, but the consequences are similar and problematic. First, the teachings of Scripture are misunderstood and the blessings they would bring are forfeited. The case for a dispensational understanding of the Bible is weakened when we base it on arguments that can't be supported from Scripture, leading people to reject the whole because of the weakness of a part. Overstating distinctions also runs the risk of drawing attention away from the aspects of dispensationalism that bring great benefit.

QUESTIONS

1. Why do you think dispensational distinctions will or will not continue into eternity?
2. What verse in Paul's letters links members of the Body of Christ to the New Jerusalem?
3. Can you identify ways in which the Bible's teaching about our eternal hope can or should affect your life as a believer?

DISPENSATIONALISM AND REFORMED THEOLOGY
Understanding the big picture can help us with the parts.

Somewhere near the end of the twentieth century interest in the study of theology declined in the local church. The reasons for that are complex, but most Christians now focus their attention on the practical matters of life and the challenges they face just getting through the day. The hair splitting that goes on in the musty offices of theologians seems irrelevant in a life already too hectic and complicated.

Church history is probably one of the few areas of study considered more irrelevant than theology. What happened 500 years ago in the middle of a small German town can't possibly have anything to do with struggles on a Saturday afternoon for the parent of a challenging teenager. That parent needs God's wisdom for how to deal with a curfew buster, not a better understanding of the Great Schism of 1054.

But both theology and church history turn out to be very relevant to the Christian life in the twenty-first century. Only with at least a minimal understanding of these two fields of study can we understand the difference between what various churches teach on questions like:

- Are Roman Catholics saved? What about people of other faiths?
- Is the Bible still authoritative, even on matters like homosexuality and a woman's role in the church?
- Has an adult child who has abandoned the church lost their salvation?
- Is there any point to prayer if God has already determined how everything will turn out?

We also need an understanding of our heritage if we're to view our faith with a perspective bigger than our immediate situation. The

history of Christianity is filled with courageous individuals who took a stand for truth,
sometimes risking their lives to do so. The example they set reminds us that any negative consequences we might experience because of our faith don't begin to measure up to their commitment to God and his Word. In Hebrews 11 we read about some of the Old Testament heroes of the faith who boldly obeyed God. Then we're told, "Therefore, since we are surrounded by so great a cloud of witnesses, let us also lay aside every weight, and sin which clings so closely, and let us run with endurance the race that is set before us" (Heb. 12:1). That same admonition can be made when we look at those who have faithfully served God and his church since that verse was written.

What follows is an extremely abbreviated and some would say simplistic overview of church history since the close of the New Testament. This brief summary can then become a framework for discussing some of the basic doctrinal developments that have resulted in the various religious groups we see today.

TWO THOUSAND YEARS OF CHURCH HISTORY IN THREE MINUTES (OK, MAYBE FOUR)

During the New Testament the church was viewed by the Roman Empire as a threat, and Christians were therefore persecuted. This got progressively worse until by the beginning of the fourth century (the 300s) the Emperor Diocletian ordered all Christian churches destroyed, all copies of the Scripture burned, and all church leaders executed.

Diocletian was followed on the throne by Constantine the Great. Tradition says Constantine converted to Christianity in 312 when, while preparing for battle, he looked up and saw the words, "In this sign, conquer!" over the image of a cross. Whether or not that story is true he went on to radically change the position of the Roman Empire regarding Christianity. Constantine returned all confiscated property to the church and decreed that all persecution end. In subsequent years he went further, funding the construction of large basilicas and granting the church tax advantages. But perhaps the greatest impact of Constantine's conversion came in 331 when he ordered that 50 copies of the Bible be produced. This marked the first time the Bible with the New Testament included was copied openly by professional scribes and may have been the point at which a formal list of books to be included in the New Testament was established.

Constantine didn't like living in Rome, so he established a new capital. He rebuilt the town of Byzantium in what is now northwest Turkey into a grand city and in a demonstration of his lack of humility renamed it Constantinople. This city (now known as Istanbul) became a second center of the Roman Empire, which, from this point in time, is sometimes called the Eastern Empire or the Byzantine Empire because of the city's older name.

This new cooperation between church and state brought real advantages for the church, including the end to brutal persecution and the spread of Scripture now copied openly and spread throughout the empire. But it didn't take long before the connection between church and state also brought very negative consequences. Constantine learned of doctrinal disputes in the Christian church about the Person of Christ and ordered that leading bishops join him at the nearby city of Nicea to settle the disagreement. The result of that meeting, or church council, was the Nicene Creed, which affirmed a very biblical view of Christ. But the precedent had been set; the state was now involved in doctrinal matters.

Over the next several centuries this connection between church and state became more intertwined. As a series of weaker men became Roman emperors and stronger men held the position of bishop in the major cities, the balance of power shifted until the church emerged as the more dominant of the two powers. The term *Holy Roman Empire* reflects this shift as things got to the point that no man had a chance of holding the position of emperor without the blessing and approval of the bishops.

Just as the empire now had a western center (Rome) and an eastern center (Constantinople), the church did also. The bishops of these two cities became the most influential of all the bishops and vied for ultimate influence within the church. This came to a head in the eleventh century when a minor doctrinal question became the justification for a split.

When the Holy Spirit came in Acts 2, was he sent by the Son (John 16:7) or by both the Son and the Father (John 6:38)? If this question strikes you as inconsequential remember that this conflict was more about power in the church than about truth. As a result, in 1054 what is now called The Great Schism took place and the church divided. The bishop and his followers in Constantinople declared that only they were fully committed to truth, so they became known as the East-

114

ern Orthodox Church. The bishop in Rome and his followers said those in
the east had forsaken the true church and they were the true and universal church centered in Rome (the word catholic comes from a Greek word meaning universal).

This explains why today groups within the Eastern Orthodox Church (for example, the Greek Orthodox and Russian Orthodox churches) and the Roman Catholic Church look alike in some ways. The things they have in common predate The Great Schism of 1054 and the differences can be traced to their separate paths after that separation. For example, the Roman Catholic rule that priests must be celibate was formally adopted in 1139, which explains why Eastern Orthodox priests can marry.

In the following centuries the Roman Catholic Church grew more powerful, and its control spread over almost every area of life throughout Europe even as the Roman Empire was collapsing. It truly was catholic; there was no church west of Constantinople except for the church centered in Rome. As almost always happens in situations like this, corruption became commonplace, amassing wealth became a central goal, and doing whatever was necessary to maintain control became acceptable. It's hard to overstate the negative impact of Roman Catholicism on the gospel and on the lives of everyone except the clergy during this period of history. There's a reason this is sometimes referred to as the Dark Ages.

Not surprisingly, the Roman Catholic Church declared that Scripture's authority was subject to the greater authority of both the Pope and the decisions of the church. Eternal life came only to those who conformed to the rules and regulations of the church, which started with the fulfillment of the seven sacraments. Every area of life from birth and the baptism of infants to death and the ordinance of last rights was subject to the control of the clergy, and the threat of excommunication and eternal damnation loomed over anyone who challenged them. Latin continued to be the language of the church long after it had died out everywhere else, and as a result the services were unintelligible to even the educated among the people. That extended to the Bible, which could only be published in Latin, thus keeping it out of the hands of the people.

In the early 1500s Martin Luther, a German priest teaching theology at a Roman Catholic university in the German town of Wittenberg, was spending time studying the Book of Romans in connection with some lectures he was to give. Romans 1:17 troubled him because it declared "The righteous will live by faith." This inner struggle over the connection between faith and righteousness came at the same time other things were weighing on his mind, including the great wealth he saw at the Vatican when he visited Rome on a trip for church business and how it contrasted with the deep poverty of the villagers around Wittenberg. In 1517 he wrote a document now known as The Ninety-five Theses. These 95 statements, many in the form of a question, challenged some of the corruption and theological error Luther saw in the church. It was not a rejection of Catholicism; Luther seems to have thought Pope Leo X must be unaware of the problems within the church. But he also wondered why the Pope didn't do things within his power according to Roman Catholic dogma, like empty purgatory and allow all those contained there to enter heaven.

The events of the next several years unfolded in a way that clearly show God's hand at work and Luther's commitment to truth while under the sentence of death. Luther went through a series of trials and was ordered to recant his writings. He refused, saying, "Unless I am convinced by the testimony of the Scriptures or by clear reason...I am bound by the Scriptures I have quoted, and my conscience is captive to the Word of God. I cannot and will not recant anything, since it is neither safe nor right to go against conscience. May God help me. Amen." Luther was declared an outlaw, his arrest ordered, and his literature banned.

On his way back to Wittenberg from that last trial Luther was "abducted" by masked men pretending to be robbers and taken to a castle belonging to Frederick III who gave Luther protection within his castle. While living there over the next several years he translated the Bible into German and wrote a massive amount of material that both criticized the Roman church and laid out a biblical view of key doctrines like salvation and eternal life.

Luther's writings and his courageous stand for truth led to what we now call the Protestant Reformation, which grew stronger and spread with each passing year. Great men of faith protested against the doctrinal and practical abuses of the Roman Catholic Church and called for it to be reformed according to the abandoned truths of Scripture. The core commitments of this movement are sometimes identified by three phrases Martin Luther proclaimed, each using the Latin word sola, meaning only or alone.

Sola scriptura, or Scripture alone, expresses the reformers' conviction that all truth must be based on the teachings of the Bible, and that the pope has no authority except when what he says aligns with Scripture.

Sola fide, faith alone, communicates that salvation comes not by obedience to the sacraments or any other set of behaviors, but only by faith.

Sola gratia, grace alone, declares that no person is ever worthy of salvation. It is only by God's grace that anyone receives eternal life.

Martin Luther's courageous stand transformed his world, and though too many Christians don't realize it, by God's grace the effect of his work shaped history down to and including the contemporary church. We typically think of today's church as a splintered and too often hostile group of denominations. But looking at them in the context of the Reformation helps us see them as major groupings, often with much more in common than we might expect.

Label words are tricky when used to describe a person or group because their meaning can be fuzzy, but they can also be helpful. For our purposes here the word evangelical will be used to describe a person or group who holds to Luther's basic affirmations. Thus, we'll define an *evangelical* as someone who accepts three things as true:

1. Jesus Christ was God come in the flesh, fully divine and fully human.
2. His death on the cross was the full payment for sin and the only means by which a person can be reconciled to God.
3. This gift of salvation is made available by God's grace and received by faith alone.

We can begin a diagram of the various theological positions with a simple circle.

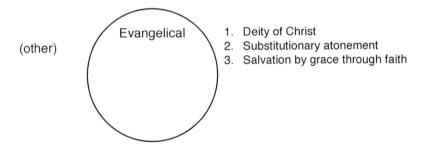

All those who reject any or all of those three truths lie outside the circle. Their theology may be what we would call liberal, rejecting the Deity of Christ, and/or believing that good works are essential to achieving eternal life. In either case these groups are not evangelicals.

Within this circle we can identify a subset we'll call fundamentalists. This word currently has both a denotation (formal definition) and a connotation (an informal use within culture). Its connotation generally describes someone who carries a big black Bible, harshly judges everyone who doesn't believe and act just like them, and is generally unhappy and unpleasant. By denotation the word *fundamentalist*, at least as we'll use it here, refers to someone who accepts the Bible as the inerrant and authoritative Word of God.

Not all evangelicals are fundamentalists, but all fundamentalists are evangelicals. Thus, we have a circle within a circle.

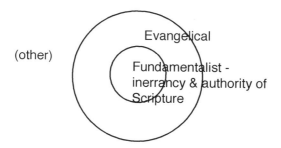

Thus, the work of Martin Luther led to what we now call evangelicalism and fundamentalism. Scripture alone, grace alone, and faith alone were the core values of the Reformation and the core commitments of our two circles in the diagram above.

Luther's commitment to truth emboldened other men, including John Calvin and Huldrych Zwingli, to join the movement protesting the doctrinal and practical abuses of the Roman Catholic Church and calling for it to be reformed according to scriptural teaching. The Protestant Reformation grew stronger and spread with each passing year.

John Calvin probably rates as Luther's equal in terms of his contribution to theological writings. He was born 26 years after Luther and died 18 years later than Luther, so they were roughly contemporaries. Calvin's central teachings having to do with salvation, now known as Calvinism, are sometimes expressed using the acrostic TULIP.

Total Depravity - each of us is completely and fully corrupted by sin and have nothing of worth before God.

Unconditional Election - God sovereignly chooses whom he will save, and there is no merit in those who are elected that causes them to be chosen by God.

119

Limited Atonement - Christ died only for those whom he elected to save.

Irresistible Grace - those God chooses will be saved. His grace cannot be resisted.

Perseverance of the Saints - the saved cannot lose their salvation but are preserved by God through to eternity.

Added together, the three solas and the five doctrines of Calvinism form what we typically refer to as Reformed theology. That term expresses the convictions of these two great men and others that the church had gone way off track and core teachings needed to be reformed and brought back into alignment with the Bible's teachings. With one exception, these theological convictions became the basis for the theology that spread across Europe and continues to characterize most of the Protestant movement today.

That one exception is the L of TULIP, limited atonement. A very sizable portion of those who identify themselves as holding to a Reformed theology reject that item of Calvin's outline and say that Christ's death provided atonement for everyone but is only applied to those who are chosen by God. Several passages, including 1 John 2:2, certainly seem to support this: "He is the propitiation for our sins, and not for ours only but also for the sins of the whole world."

Besides Reformed theology, other changes came with the Protestant Reformation that affected every area of life. The Bible was translated into the language of the people, wherever they lived, so it could be read to them and they could understand. Church services were also conducted in the local language with the congregation singing hymns instead of the Roman Catholic service in which only the choir sang in Latin. Luther denounced the view of the Roman church that only the clergy did work that had value before God and declared that all work is worship if done for God and therefore has value. This became known as the Protestant work ethic and by extension taught that all work should be done diligently since it was done before God. The Reformation affected finances as economies in Europe stopped sending massive amounts of money to Rome, politics as the clergy lost their influence over who governed at all levels of society, and education as universities were no longer extensions of the church.

The Roman Catholic Church certainly fought back against the reformers. This conflict was most intense in countries where the Roman church had the greatest influence with the state and developed into what is now referred to as the Inquisition. In Spain and Portugal the persecutions were every bit as cruel as those of Diocletian.

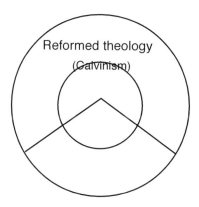

For about the first century after the publication of Luther's Ninety-five Theses in 1517 the Protestant church and its leaders focused primarily on the recovery of the core truths of our faith, and the doctrines of salvation as outlined above. But gradually theologians turned their attention to other doctrines including how we should read and understand the Bible.

The emergence of two divergent schools of thought was more gradual than the fairly abrupt and sudden beginning of the Protestant Reformation, but eventually the lines were drawn between what we now call Covenant theology and Dispensational theology. The basic differences between them are discussed in Understanding Your Bible and have to do with hermeneutics - the interpretation of Scripture.

Covenant theology adopted an allegorical hermeneutic that believes there is one people of God, referred to as Israel in the Old Testament and the Body of Christ in the New Testament. What appear to be contradictions between what is said to those groups are best explained by interpreting what is said to Israel as a spiritual allegory that should be understood metaphorically. This is especially true regarding passages about the future and God's plans for his people.

Dispensational theology uses a literal hermeneutic and as a result understands the Bible to teach that God dealt with Israel as his special people but has now set them aside, albeit temporarily, to deal with all people without regard for their nationality. At some point in the future after the rapture God will resume his dealings with Israel and literally fulfill all his promises to them including establishing a kingdom on earth in which Christ the Messiah will rule from Jerusalem.

Just as the Protestant Reformation spread across Europe but took hold in some countries more firmly than others, so these two schools of theology each had a greater presence in some regions than others. Covenant theology became more prominent in Germany, the Netherlands, and central Europe. Dispensational theology became the norm in England, Scotland and, to a lesser degree, Scandinavia. But both Covenant theology and Dispensational theology fall within the category of Reformed theology.

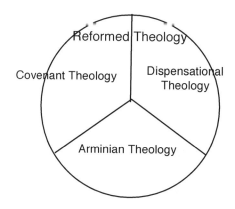

IMPLICATIONS AND APPLICATIONS

Most countries have days set aside to remember the great men and women of their history, individuals who made possible, often at considerable personal sacrifice, the good things enjoyed in contemporary life. Those memorials remind us that believers owe those who went before us a debt of gratitude and that their example should motivate us to faithful service. Unfortunately, too many Christians have very little knowledge of the commitment and sacrifices of men like Martin Luther, William Tyndale, and John Wycliffe. These courageous leaders worked to recapture key truths of the faith, gave us the Bible and church services in our own language, and took the gospel to places it had not reached. They wrote great hymns of the faith (Luther and Wesley), powerful expositions of Scripture (Luther and Calvin), and, for the first time in centuries, translated the Bible into the language of the people so they could read it for themselves (John Wycliffe and William Tyndale).

It's unfortunate most Christians today know nothing of these courageous individuals, many of whom were martyred for their commitment to
the Bible and its truth. They set a humbling example of dedication to what matters from an eternal perspective, a model that would serve us well in an age of immediacy and self-absorption.

This understanding of church history also reminds us of that which unites us as believers. Anyone who accepts the commitments of evangelicalism is part of the Body of Christ and therefore a brother or sister in the faith. Those within the circle of fundamentalists may come to different conclusions about the interpretation of Scripture, but our acceptance of it as God's inspired and inerrant Word puts us in agreement regarding its authority in matters of doctrine and practice.

The hostility that characterized some of the disagreements within the history of the Protestant church is a blot on the record of God's children. In light of the persecution Martin Luther and those who bravely followed in his footsteps suffered, which in some cases included martyrdom at the hands of a false church, animosity over matters of hermeneutics seems especially inappropriate. I can hold to a dispensational interpretation of Scripture and at the same time value fellowship with those who adopt the allegorical hermeneutic of Covenant theology. What we have in common, especially if we fall within the categories of fundamentalism and Reformed theology, easily outweighs our differences. If I can't worship and serve alongside someone with whom I share those core commitments, I need to reexamine my spiritual maturity.

QUESTIONS

1. Why is it called the Protestant Reformation?
2. On what date did Martin Luther post his Ninety-five Theses that began the Reformation?
3. What are the five points of classic Calvinism?
4. What is your opinion regarding the third point?

WHAT ABOUT THAT THIRD SEGMENT OF THE CIRCLE?

As too often happens, the disagreement about matters of theology, in this case hermeneutics, became the basis for denouncing the other side as heretics and in some extreme cases led to persecution. On both sides of the issue the focus turned to an emphasis on the theological distinctions with sermons and writings often characterized by a harsh and critical tone. Individuals from both Covenant theology and Dispensational theology were guilty of inappropriate conduct.

In 1729 a small group of young men in Oxford, England, grew increasingly dissatisfied with what they saw as a cold, sterile, and too often critical spirit within the Church of England. They decided to meet several times each week to focus on prayer, Bible reading, and their commitment to live for God every hour of every day. This included caring for the poo, and lonely, for prisoners, and orphans. They believed by doing the simple things of the gospel they could have a living, vibrant relationship with God instead of what they saw as the academic and lifeless religion around them.

This group of four to six men were mockingly called *The Holy Club* by their peers, and *methodists* because, their critics said, they thought they could achieve a higher level of spirituality by following a regimen of behaviors.

Brothers Charles and John Wesley and George Whitefield were among that first group, which rapidly grew and spread as their interest in spiritual vitality touched a nerve with the population in England and eventually beyond. What resulted is now known as the Methodist Revival; their commitment to preaching and missionary work caused it quickly spread across England and, in the late 1700s, to the United States.

This movement became almost anti-theology, reacting against what they saw as the sterility that resulted from the path Reformed theology had taken. But to the extent the movement expressed a theology it came to be the antithesis of Calvinism. You can go down the TULIP acrostic and accurately describe Methodist Theology, also known as Wesleyan theology or Arminian theology, by identifying the opposite.

Instead of total depravity, Wesleyan theology teaches that each person is born with what's called *prevenient grace* (grace that precedes the hearing of the gospel), which is sufficient to allow the free will of the individual to respond to the gospel if and when they hear it.

Unconditional election is countered with the doctrine of conditional election in which God chooses for salvation those he knows through his omniscience will accept him with their free will. Limited atonement is, as you
would expect, replaced with an unlimited offer of salvation to all mankind. Irresistible grace instead becomes resistible grace whereby the individual in his or her free will can reject the work of the Holy Spirit and the offer of salvation.

The perseverance of the saints, or eternal security, is countered with conditional preservation. God will preserve the believer who continues in the faith. Thus, those who turn their backs on the gospel or refuses to live consistent with its standards loses their salvation and must again repent and accept the gift of salvation.

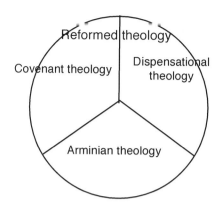

In the roughly 300 years since the Holy Club began meeting in Oxford there have been too many splits and divisions within various Christian groups to track. Many of those splits had nothing to do with theology but occurred because of disagreements about sometimes very minor matters of practice. Any list of current denominations and church groups would fill a book and that book only gets thicker. Despite a growing disinterest in theology Christians continue to have trouble getting along with each other.

If, however, we try to identify the general theological position of any particular evangelical denomination we could put it in one of two, and then into one of three categories. The first category would be either within or outside of Reformed theology. That is, does the group's theology generally align with the tenets of Calvinism? As noted above, many who describe themselves as Calvinists do not hold to a limited atonement but do agree with the other four items.

The vast majority of those who are either covenant or dispensational in their theology are also Reformed. Regarding the basic matters related to salvation—depravity, election, and eternal security—they align with Calvin. The other category describing those who do not hold to Reformed theology is
often referred to as Arminian theology after Jacobus Arminius, who wrote many books in opposition to the teaching of John Calvin. The

roughly equivalent terms Wesleyan theology and Methodist theology probably aren't as helpful because they tend to suggest a denomination instead of a school of theology that includes both.

The next level of categories describes how a particular group views the interpretation of Scripture. It is here we distinguish between covenant and dispensational theology and their use of the allegorical or literal hermeneutic respectively. (Again, see Understanding Your Bible for a more complete discussion of this.)

Where does Arminian theology fall on the issue of hermeneutics? Is it covenant or dispensational in its approach to the Bible? That question is difficult to answer in part because of the history of this branch of evangelicalism. The Holy Club began as a reaction to what those men saw as the cold, sterile Christianity of Reformed theology, so their emphasis was on living a life of discipleship—on actions, not doctrines and hermeneutics. But generally, Arminian theology has aligned with Covenant theology. This is in part because the practices of many groups within the Wesleyan tradition, which include speaking in tongues and healings, are best supported with passages applying to God's dealings with Israel. An allegorical hermeneutic that sees only one people of God throughout history can more easily bring practices from God's work with Israel into this age.

Thus, we can begin by asking if a particular group or denomination is Reformed or Arminian (Wesleyan) in its theology. The former will largely align with the writings of Martin Luther and John Calvin while the latter will reject especially the tenets of Calvin. Then we can ask if a group holding to Reformed theology is covenant or dispensational in their understanding of Scripture.

We began this section by asking a series of questions relevant to contemporary life and hotly debated even within the church. Different denominations and organizations that identify themselves as evangelical will give contradictory answers to these and other issues facing believers in the twenty-first century and openly criticize opposing views as inconsistent with the faith. How can there be so much divergence and hostility? The answer comes when we understand the major divisions of evangelicalism outlined above. When that happens the perspective of a given group can be seen in the context of its core commitments and view of Scripture.

Before we go further we should note the difference between dogma and a person's personal views. The word *dogma* refers to the official position of a particular group, in this case a denomination or other religious organization. However, it's not uncommon for an individual within that organization to hold views very different from its church's dogma. Remember, Martin Luther was still a Roman Catholic priest when he came to understand the three truths expressed by his *sola* statements. The dogma of the Roman Catholic Church regarding salvation remains essentially unchanged since the days of Luther, but it is entirely possible for an individual within that church, even a priest, to be genuinely saved through faith in Christ's substitutionary death. The Roman Catholic Church is not evangelical, but someone who identifies as a Catholic might be.

This reminds us that labels are indeed risky and that our charge is to both recognize the sometimes dangerous errors of a group's dogma and the spiritual condition of any individual within that group. To denounce the error of a group must not lead to the demonization of all individuals within that group. We must listen carefully and attentively to what a person says about their beliefs without automatically overlaying the position of their group association on them.

The overview we've given above helps us understand the dynamics at work within the large group that would claim the name Christian. More than 100 years ago some prominent denominations—sometimes referred to as mainline denominations—abandoned the core commitments that define evangelicalism. In the first half of the twentieth century the leadership of these denominations decided, often to the surprise of the people in their churches, that Jesus was not God incarnate and that his death on the cross was not essential to eternal life. If the core commitments of evangelicalism are absent the questions we listed must be decided on some other basis than sola Scriptura. Questions regarding an individual's salvation become especially critical. Thus, "are Roman Catholics saved?" must be answered with a no if we respond with the dogma of that church.

- Is the Bible still authoritative, even on matters like homosexuality and a woman's role in the church?

That question will be answered differently by individuals within and without the fundamentalist circle as described above. The person who accepts the inerrancy and authority of Scripture typically answers yes, though there are certainly fundamentalists who would disagree based on their interpretation of relevant passages. The individual who is an evangelical but not a fundamentalist will probably quickly respond in the negative regarding these issues. There's very little purpose in the two of them debating the question because they come at it with very different premises. As a result it's common for the two perspectives to get very frustrated with what seems like foolishness (or worse) from the other side of the conversation.

- Has an adult child who has abandoned the church lost their salvation?

The group or individual who accepts the tenets of Reformed theology says that person, if truly a believer, has not and cannot lose their salvation. At this point it may be helpful to note another distinction that becomes clearer with the description and diagrams we've given above.

The term *creedal* church is used to describe a denomination that expresses its doctrinal commitments in terms of the creeds the church has written over the centuries. Earlier in this section we referred to the meeting, or church council, that Constantine called in 325 to settle disputes over the person of Christ. This council produced the document now known as the Nicene Creed, which states the orthodox view of Christ's deity. The best known of the creeds is the Apostle's

Creed, which probably dates to the late 300s. These and other creeds written at church councils were widely circulated in the early church as a way to teach believers the core doctrinal truths of Christianity and so were written with an "I believe...." format. It thus became easy for some denominations to express their commitments by saying, "We hold to the Apostle's Creed, the Nicene Creed...." etc. It's not that they place the creeds above the Bible, but they use them as an efficient way to express what they understand to be biblical teaching. Unfortunately, the effect of using the creeds to state a denomination's beliefs can have an unintended and undesirable effect, namely, to focus attention on a creedal statement instead of the teachings of Scripture. When a denomination's literature says, "We believe..." and cites one of the historical church's creeds instead of "The Bible teaches..." the result can too often be that an individual looks to the church and its decrees as the authority instead of Scripture. The historical creeds of the church have continued value as a concise statement of the core commitments of the faith, but if they replace Scripture as the foundation the church is not well served.

Returning to the question of losing one's salvation, the teachings of Scripture are clear. Salvation is a gift from God given unconditionally by his grace. It is entirely his work in us from before the foundations of the world (Eph. 1:4) and maintained by him until eternity (Phil. 1:6). A more complete discussion of this truth is outside the purposes of this book, but in the context of this chapter it may be helpful to note that eternal security is a doctrinal commitment of those within the segment of our diagram labeled Reformed theology.

- Is there any point to prayer if God has already determined how everything will turn out?

This critical question touches on one of the central disciplines of the Christian life. Prayer, including bringing our requests before the throne of grace (Heb. 4:16), is an almost instinctive part of being a child of God. We are blessed to have a lot of clear teaching in Scripture on the topic of prayer that guides us in every aspect of the privilege of coming before God at any time in complete openness. But the question about the efficacy of prayer, the point of asking God for anything, presents itself to any Christian who accepts the commitment of Reformed theology to the biblical truth of God's total sovereignty over all events (Eph. 1:11). If God has indeed determined the course of all things both great and small, what is the point of asking him to do anything? Isn't it already decided? This logical difficulty has led many to reject either the absolute sovereignty of God or the efficacy of prayer. But a third option exists.

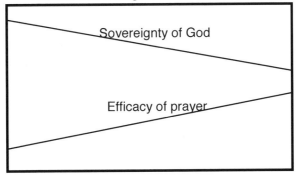

In the above diagram the box represents the sum total of all humanity's knowledge and understanding. Note that the box accurately displays the most important truth about human comprehension, namely, that it is finite. All the mental ability of all humans throughout all of history, both realized and unrealized, is finite.

The two lines represent the biblical truths of the sovereignty of God and the fact that God responds to the prayers of his people. For the purposes of this illustration the point of intersection of those two lines, which seem contradictory and mutually exclusive, is the point at which they are reconciled. One of the axioms of geometry is that two non-parallel lines on the same plane will intersect. In this illustration we note the point of intersection is outside the limits of human comprehension.

132

The Bible clearly teaches God is sovereign over all things, he controls all actions, events, and outcomes, and has determined all of it since before the foundations of the world. This truth is presented in both direct statements (Eph. 1:11; Isa. 46:8-11; Dan. 4:35) and seen in a long list of narrative sections (Gen. 7:4; Dan. 4:17,25,32; Num. 14:26-30).

Scripture also clearly teaches that God answers the prayers of his saints. One of the most powerful of those passages is James 5 where we read, "The prayer of a righteous person has great power as it is working" (v. 16). James goes on to illustrate this truth with a reference to Elijah, "a man with a nature like ours, and he prayed fervently that it might not rain, and for three years and six months it did not rain on the earth. Then he prayed again, and heaven gave rain, and the earth bore its fruit" (vv. 17-18). The withholding and return of rain is tied directly to Elijah's prayer. In Colossians 4:3 Paul asks those believers to pray he would have opportunity to proclaim the truth with clarity. Why would Paul ask them to pray for him if those prayers had no effect? And in Philippians 1:19 Paul is sure of his deliverance because of their prayers and the help of the Spirit, an indication he considered both to be effective forces. I cannot explain or understand how the sovereignty of God and the effectiveness of prayer align, but I don't have to.

The Bible says both that God chose those he saves before the foundations of the world (Eph. 1:4) and that the receiving of salvation is through the individual's exercise of faith (Eph. 2:8). Without faith it is impossible to please God, an admonition given to believers about their Christian life (Heb. 11:6). If the Bible teaches these two seemingly mutually exclusive truths—God's sovereign control over all things and my free will in choosing—then I will accept them both.

Many Christians have trouble doing that and end up either denying one or the other truth or bending one of the diagram's lines so the point of intersection is within the bounds of their understanding thus altering the clear teaching of Scripture. The sovereignty of God is understood to be nothing more than his foreknowledge or the effectiveness of prayer limited to the calming effect it has on the believer.

If we say we are committed to the principle of sola Scriptura then we have to allow it to speak with authority and accept the Bible's teaching when it exceeds our ability to fully grasp what it teaches. Indeed, I should expect that the wisdom of God will surpass mine, especially when it comes to the ways of God. That was the thrust of God's questions to Job at the end of that powerful book and is expressed again in 1 Corinthians 2:16: "For who has understood the mind of the Lord so as to instruct him?"

The diagram we've used to illustrate the twin truths of God's sovereignty and prayer's effectiveness can also be used for other questions. The sovereignty of God has determined all things from eternity yet obedience brings blessing and disobedience discipline (Deut. 5:33). This is another example of the same dynamic.

IMPLICATIONS AND APPLICATIONS

The contents of this chapter don't relate directly to Dispensational theology but deal with what is called historical theology. However, one of the charges sometimes brought against a dispensational understanding of Scripture is that it is both a recent development and an artificial system laid over the Bible instead of contained within it. In light of those criticisms it's helpful to have a general overview of church history. Then we can see that because of the almost universal influence of the Roman Catholic Church for centuries the truths of Scripture were effectively lost until the early 1500s. The next century was spent recovering the truths of salvation expressed in Luther's sola statements and related issues as reflected in Calvin's writings. Only after the basic doctrines of the faith were brought back into alignment with Scripture did the church turn its attention to matters of hermeneutics.

Just as Luther recaptured the biblical truth of *sola fide* regarding salvation we must understand the role of faith in accepting the teachings of Scripture. It is evidence of an inclination to the sin of pride that we will so easily reject or alter the Bible's clear declarations when they don't fit with what we think makes sense. Sola scriptura is as applicable to doctrines of the Christian life as it is to the Bible's teachings on salvation. In an age when human wisdom is exalted to an unprecedented degree the Christian is called to humbly accept the Word of God as our final authority on matters of doctrine and practice.

When accepted in humble faith the teaching of Scripture on the difficult questions of the Christian life can bring peace, if not full understanding. Trusting God's sovereignty over all things brings a confidence that he does, indeed, "work for the good of those who love him, who have been called according to his purpose" (Rom. 8:28).

QUESTIONS

1. What names are given to the groups opposed to Reformed theology?
2. How do these groups respond to each of the five points of Calvinism?
3. Using the Internet look for a list of key leaders in the Protestant Reformation and learn about one of them.

APPLYING MID-ACTS DISPENSATIONALISM
Putting its principles to work

Thus far our focus has been on several theological issues associated with mid-Acts dispensationalism, and we've tried to make clear that each of these has practical implications. For example, the question of the dispensational position of believers who lived across the change from the dispensation of Law to the dispensation of Grace determines how we read and understand the Hebrew-Christian epistles and the Gospels. A careful understanding of what the Bible says about eschatology can bring confidence and joy as we consider the great future God has for all believers regardless of the dispensation in which they lived their earthly life. Understanding our common roots in the Protestant Reformation reminds us that what we have in common as evangelical fundamentalists far exceeds any differences that may exist between us.

In addition to these issues the thoughtful Bible student will soon realize there are other questions that are best answered only with the application of a careful, mid-Acts dispensational framework. In this section we'll raise some of those practical questions and try to rigorously apply what we've learned. In some cases the results may be a bit surprising.

REGARDING OUR SUPPORT FOR A PARTICULAR NATION

When the modern state of Israel was established in 1948 many evangelical Christians saw a special reason for celebrating. The book of Revelation is clear that Israel exists as a nation during the tribulation, which dispensationalists see as the next event in God's eschatological agenda following the rapture. They therefore viewed the establishment of the state of Israel as an indication that we are now closer to the rapture. The stage is set.

Add to this the dispensationalist's conviction that the Jews are God's special people and Israel his favored nation (Ex. 19:5-6) and support for the current state of Israel quickly became a staple of evangelicalism, especially in the United States. Israel has no greater advocate in the U.S. than the evangelical voter and any politician who hopes to get the backing of evangelicals had better have a record of support for the nation of Israel. To suggest that Israel has acted inappropriately in any situation is a risky thing for a politician who will almost certainly be severely criticized by the evangelical community where support for that country is often seen as a matter of spiritual and political orthodoxy.

A case can certainly be made that the current state of Israel is a key strategic ally of the United States. It is the only democracy in the Middle East and has been supportive of U.S. interests in that volatile part of the world. But apart from very practical reasons for a close relationship with the nation of Israel it is not possible, within the context of biblical teaching, to make a case for unwavering and unquestioning support for that nation. This is especially true for the dispensationalist.

One of the core principles of dispensationalism is that God does not now have a special people or nation. The biblical nation of Israel was set aside by God because of their unbelief (Rom. 11:20), and there is now no distinction between Jew and Gentile (Col. 3:11). In this dispensation God does not have a favored nation. Rather he deals with individuals on the basis of their response to Jesus Christ. The current state of Israel is a political entity with no spiritual connection to the nation chosen by God to be the center of his work in the world. Orthodox Judaism, which exerts influence over all aspects of life in Israel, is openly hostile to Christianity and thus God's work in the world, and certainly rejects Jesus as the Messiah and Savior. Modern-day Israel is a political state, a nation no different from any other nation in terms of its relationship with God, precisely because God does not now have a special connection to any nation.

Nor can a case be made that the rapture is in any sense nearer or more likely to occur because Israel now exists as a nation. As we demonstrated in the
section on eschatology, until late in his ministry Paul expected the rapture to happen in his lifetime (1 Thess. 4:15). For this reason, and because no event is a necessary precursor to the rapture, we describe the rapture as being imminent; it can happen at any time. It was imminent prior to 1948 and cannot be more imminent now. The rapture would not be less imminent if for some reason the current state of Israel failed, ceased to exist. Again, as we noted in the section on eschatology, there may very well be a generation between the rapture and the beginning of the tribulation, more than enough time for a new and different state of Israel to emerge.

All of this reminds us that the same standards we apply to the conduct of other nations should apply equally to Israel and that they should receive no special treatment if it is based on some supposed connection with the Old Testament nation. Like all governments they sometimes act in accordance with biblical standards of righteousness and justice and sometimes do not. We do well to keep in mind that current Israel is a secular state and that its existence has no bearing on the likelihood of the rapture occurring in the near future.

A similar line of thinking may be helpful as we consider a biblical view of our attitude toward our own country. In the dispensation of Grace God works with those individuals who accept his gracious gift of salvation by faith alone. Those who do are made members of one Body without regard to ethnicity or national origin. God does not now have a favored nation or a special people.

Patriotism, when defined as devotion and support for one's country, is both natural and appropriate. Patriotism becomes problematic when it moves toward the view that God looks with special favor on a particular country. American evangelicals in particular have tended to view their country as the object of God's unique blessing compared to other nations and therefore superior to other countries.

In James 1:17 we read, "Every good gift and every perfect gift is from above, coming down from the Father of lights, with whom there is no variation or shadow due to change." Thus we correctly conclude God has blessed the U.S. with rich natural resources, a beautiful and varied landscape, an enduring democracy, and economic prosperity. But the rapidly declining moral standards of American culture remind us that American society is no more righteous than some other countries, many of which are equally blessed with natural beauty. The concept of American exceptionalism may make for good politics but it's bad theology in the dispensation of Grace.

REGARDING PRAYER

Many contrasts exist between the dispensation of Law and the dispensation of Grace, some of them important to the daily life of the believer. Examples include the observance of holy days, dietary regulations, and ceremonies. Some mid-Acts dispensationalists have identified prayer as another area where God's instructions for his people under the dispensation of Law differ significantly from those to members of the Body of Christ. This seems like a reasonable conclusion because of some of the striking things Christ said to his disciples during his earthly ministry.

If two of them agree in prayer on anything, God will give them what they ask for (Matt. 18:19). John 14:13-14 says, "And I will do whatever you ask in my name, so that the Father may be glorified in the Son. If you ask me anything in my name, I will do it." In Mark 11:24 we read, "Whatever you ask for, believe that you have received it, and it will be yours."

These promises stand in contrast to what we read in Paul's letters about prayer. In 2 Corinthians 12: 8-9 Paul writes about the thorn in the flesh (probably a problem with his eyes) that plagued him. He writes, "I asked the Lord three times about this, that it would depart from me. But he said to me, 'My grace is enough for you.'"

Based on the promises from Christ to the disciples Paul should have been healed. He certainly would have asked in faith, undoubtedly had others who also prayed for his healing, and would have prayed in Christ's name. So why wasn't he healed? Many have concluded the dynamics of prayer—how they should be offered and how God responds—differ in the dispensation of Law, the context of Christ's teachings, and in the current dispensation of Grace. It's said that as members of the Body of Christ we will be frustrated and disappointed if we expect God to respond to our prayers as he promised the disciples he would respond.

However, these conclusions result from reading Christ's teaching on prayer too casually. The need for a closer look at his instructions on the topic comes when we ask ourselves if it could ever really work like those verses seem to suggest. Was there, or will there ever be, a time when just because something is prayed in faith (Mk. 11:24), "in Jesus' name" (Jn. 14:13-14), or by two believers in agreement (Matt. 18:19) the request will automatically be granted? That turns prayer into nothing more than a spell, an incantation that, when recited in just the right way by the right number of people, guarantees a yes answer.

If it worked like that the disciples certainly would have prayed that Christ come down from the cross or that the Jews receive the offer of the kingdom in the early chapters of Acts. Indeed, they probably did pray both of those and more without the desired response from God. Yet their faith and commitment were not shaken. Why? Because they fully understood Christ's teaching on prayer.

They understood that no single part of Christ's teaching on a subject could be isolated from his other instructions on the topic. In Matthew 6:10 Christ taught them to pray for God's will to be done, something he modeled in the garden when he prayed, "Not what I will, but what you will" (Matt. 26:39). The disciples knew the priority of God's will outranked their desires.

The disciples also knew to follow that most basic principle of interpretation: consider the context. Too many have pulled out one phrase from John 14, "Whatever you ask in my name this I will do" (v. 13) without including the rest of that sentence or the next. Christ adds, "that the Father may be glorified in the Son." This taught the disciples and reminds us the Father's glory is the highest priority and anything not leading to that end won't happen. In verse 14 he says, "If you ask me anything in my name I will do it." They certainly understood the words, "in my name" were not part of a magical incantation, necessary words in a spell, but rather that the request had to be consistent with what Christ himself would ask of the Father.

The disciples also brought a level of common sense to Christ's teaching too often missing from some of today's readers. In Luke 11:5-13 he taught the disciples about prayer using the story of a man who went to his neighbor at midnight asking for three loaves of bread to feed an unexpected guest. The neighbor refused the request and only relented because of the man's persistence (v. 8).

A similar passage is found in Luke 18:1-8 where a widow pesters a reluctant judge who neither fears God nor respects men (v. 4) but gave her justice only because she kept bothering him (v. 5). Was Christ teaching the disciples that a reluctant God requires pestering? Or did they understand the key point, that the believer should not hesitate to come repeatedly to the Father with the burdens of the heart?

The content of the prayers of God's people varies from one dispensation to another. Jews in the dispensation of Law prayed for complete victory going into battle for land given them by God and for the arrival of the promised Messiah to rule in Jerusalem. Members of the Body of Christ pray for the spread of the gospel and the rapture. But the basic dynamics of prayer—how we pray and how God responds—are horizontal, remaining the same from one dispensation to the next.

This has important practical implications for members of the Body of Christ. Ignoring Christ's instructions on prayer causes us to miss out on important truths God wants his people to know so that our prayers are more effective. Paul's letters include many prayers that serve as examples for us, but his instructions on the topic are limited (see Phil. 4:6 and 1 Thess. 5:17). This makes Christ's teachings especially valuable.

The disciples said, "Teach us to pray" (Lk. 11:1). We also need to learn about this central element of the Christian life and can receive great benefit from the instructions Christ gave them. From the Gospels we learn that our requests must place God's interests above our own and that corporate prayer and persistence in prayer touch God's heart. To ignore this rich source of instruction on prayer because it was given to those under the dispensation of Law is a misapplication of the dispensational approach and deprives us of the benefit of the Bible's teaching on an important area of the believer's relationship with our Father.

REGARDING THE FOURTH COMMANDMENT

The Law given to Moses contains three sections: the ceremonial law, governing Israel's worship including sacrifices, holy days, and the tabernacle; the civil law, specifying the punishment for various crimes; and the moral law, laying out the basic ethical standards for life. The moral law is contained in the Ten Commandments found in Exodus 20:1-7 and Deuteronomy 5:7-21.

The ceremonial law is clearly intended for the dispensation of Law, applying to Israel in the dispensation of Law. Paul's letters make it clear the Body of Christ is not bound by those commands (see Rom. 14:1-12 and 1 Tim. 4:1-4 as examples of his instructions in this area). The if/then civil law (if someone does this then the punishment shall be...) suggests a starting point for considering matters of crime and punishment but applying the specifics of the Mosaic civil law simply does not work in contemporary culture. Israel was a theocratic and agricultural society with most of the population living in relatively isolated rural areas and sharing a common cultural heritage. This produced a society with very different conditions and needs than contemporary society.

What about the moral law, the Ten Commandments? Are they horizontal, applying since their giving at Mt. Sinai through all subsequent dispensations, or only applied within the dispensation of Law?

This question is answered fairly easily with regard to nine of the Ten Commandments. No one seriously questions if bowing down to an idol or murder still qualify as sin. The difficulty comes with the fourth commandment to keep the Sabbath. In Romans 14:5 Paul writes, "One person esteems one day as better than another, while another esteems all days alike. Each one should be fully convinced in his own mind." And he wrote to the Colossian church, "Therefore let no one pass judgment on you in questions of food and drink, or with regard to a festival or a new moon or a Sabbath. These are a shadow of the things to come, but the substance belongs to Christ" (Col. 2:16-17).

While these two passages seem to make it clear the commandment regarding the Sabbath does not apply in the dispensation of Grace, a couple of things encourage us to take a closer look. First, it seems odd that only one of the 10 should be vertical. It's almost as though the fourth commandment belongs in the ceremonial division of the Law. Also, the command to keep the Sabbath has its origins in God's act of creation, the text of the commandment making that connection. "For in six days the Lord made heaven and earth, the sea, and all that is in them, and rested on the seventh day. Therefore, the Lord blessed the Sabbath day and made it holy" (Ex. 20:11). Much as Paul's writing cites creation in support of the differing roles of male and female (see 1 Tim. 2:12-15), so the text of the fourth commandment cites creation as the basis for the prohibition of work on the Sabbath. This suggests a principle more timeless than one dispensation's command. What, then, should we do with the Sabbath?

At the very least we can agree that the observance of a particular day of the week over the others cannot be made a behavioral standard for the Christian life. The two Pauline passages mentioned above make that clear.

That said, it's worth noting that the Colossians passage is probably not a reference to the kind of Sabbath keeping directed by the fourth commandment. The believers in Colossae were apparently being pressured to conform to a set of standards even more restrictive than the Mosaic code, an unbiblical legalistic system being taught as the measure of spirituality. Paul mentions, "questions of food and drink." The Mosaic law had no restrictions on matters of drink except for the Nazirite vow, which prohibited any alcoholic drink for the duration of the vow. This indicates the problem Paul addresses is not normal Judaism. There existed in the Colossian church a group of legalistic teachers who had created a set of standards that bore a resemblance to the Law

148

but went well beyond its prohibitions. We don't know what their code said about the Sabbath but it could well have included requirements beyond those in the Law. A similar nonbiblical legalistic code apparently existed where Timothy served, which is why Paul warned him about those who insisted on celibacy (1 Tim. 4:2).

What should we do with a commandment based on God's creative work long before Mt. Sinai and placed alongside nine other commands clearly horizontal in nature, one Paul says should not be made the basis of judgment (Rom. 14:5)? Perhaps the answer is found in the words of Christ, who said, "The Sabbath was made for man, not man for the Sabbath" (Mk. 2:27).

God created man with a need for regular rest from the normal labors of life. It's noteworthy that the fourth commandment doesn't specify what work must not be done. The Pharisees did what legalists do and tried to define this commandment in ridiculous detail, which Christ said missed the whole point of God's directive—man's well-being.

So perhaps it's best to understand the fourth commandment as indicating just how important God considers our need for regular rest to be. He told Israel their rest must occur on the seventh day, while Paul tells us we should not be judged regarding one day or another. Christ teaches us a Sabbath rest is for our good and meets a basic human need, a need that exists regardless of the dispensation.

Our need for a Sabbath rest doesn't get the attention it probably should in the contemporary church, especially in the mid-Acts dispensationalist church. While Paul makes it clear Sabbath observance should not be a standard for judging, several factors—that the Sabbath is based on God's model at creation, is placed alongside timeless moral principles in the Ten Commandments, and is "made for man" (Mk. 2:27)—demonstrate the continuing value of taking one day each week for rest and restoration.

REGARDING THE DOCTRINES AND PRACTICES OF THE CHURCH

Individuals committed to mid-Acts dispensationalism who attend a church with the same perspective should have no conflict on matters like water baptism, tithing, and communion. Many of us who hold to a mid-Acts dispensational interpretation, however, cannot attend a church that shares our theological convictions. This raises the question of how we should view these issues relative to our participation in a church with a different perspective. Some allowance will be necessary if we're going to fellowship and serve with other members in the Body of Christ, but where should lines be drawn? At what point does the extent of our disagreement rise to the level of a barrier to fellowship and service?

We should first understand that fellowship and service with other believers is an essential part of God's design for every believer. Nowhere in the epistles does Paul even imagine a situation in which a Christian is not part of a local church except in a case where church discipline has required their exclusion. The number of passages in which Paul addresses doctrinal issues within a church shows disagreements are to be expected. Some of those disagreements involved matters on which he would not tolerate deviation from clear truth, including anything that touched on salvation by grace apart from any work on man's part (see Gal. 1:6-9). In other cases he urged tolerance and acceptance of differing opinions (see Rom. 14:1-4). Thus, determining if full fellowship in a church with different theological convictions is appropriate involves a careful understanding of both that church's position and a thorough grasp of scriptural teaching on the topic (Acts 17:11).

We should also understand that a decision on attending and serving a particular church may involve not only doctrinal issues but an individual's life situation. The parents of preteens may decide a greater degree of difference between their convictions and those of a church can be overlooked for the sake of their children's spiritual welfare. As we'll see, especially on the matter of water baptism, a variety of views is possible, some more problematic than others.

A church that believes water baptism is part of God's design for the local church can see that practice in a range of ways. For some congregations water baptism is essential for salvation, and apart from that ceremony a person cannot be saved. This clearly introduces personal works into a salvation that Scripture says is only received through faith and is therefore a practice that would be rejected by Paul (see Eph. 2:9; Gal. 2:15-16).

At another church water baptism is a public profession of faith in Christ's atoning work that is viewed as appropriate, even desirable, but not essential to fellowship or service. Water baptism is practiced but not stressed and is not a prerequisite to full participation in the life of the church.

In between these two positions on the spectrum is the church that does not view water baptism as essential to salvation but does require it for membership and/or serving in the church. The ceremony is stressed and seen as a standard of Christian obedience without which the believer cannot be walking in full fellowship with God or his people.

An overview of the Bible's teaching on water baptism can be found in Understanding Your Bible and will not be repeated here. The question in this context is how a mid-Acts dispensationalist should respond to the practice of water baptism in a local church and what effect, if any, that should have on their participation.

It's easiest to identify how Paul would respond to the position that water baptism is essential for salvation. Ephesians 2:8-9 makes it clear that salvation is a gift from God bestowed by his grace and that any effort on our part is excluded. "For by works of the law no human being will be justified in his sight, since through the law comes knowledge of sin" (Rom. 3:20). In Galatians 1:9 Paul says, "As we have said before, so now I say again. If anyone is preaching to you a gospel contrary to the one you received, let him be accursed."

We also have an indication how Paul would answer those who require water baptism for full participation in the church. In Galatians 5 he seems to have shifted his focus from the Judaizers, who required circumcision for salvation, to those who made it a requirement for full fellowship, and his response is the same. His readers have freedom in Christ but are at risk of submitting again to a yoke of slavery (v. 1). Paul tells the Galatian believers that if they accept the need for circumcision as urged by the false teachers, "Christ will be of no advantage to you" (v. 2) and they are "obligated to keep the whole law" (v. 3). Paul's warning not to judge others about behaviors not specifically proscribed or prescribed by God (Rom. 14:1-12) would also apply here.

Thus, the church that requires water baptism as a prerequisite to full fellowship or service violates Paul's instructions in Galatians. They have imposed a standard with no biblical support, and that introduces a degree of legalism to the Christian life.

What about the church that practices water baptism but does not make it a standard of fellowship? Is that deviation from a mid-Acts perspective a barrier to attendance and service? Several passages suggest the answer is no.

Again, Paul's Romans 14 section on nonessential matters seems to apply in this case. The priority of peace should prevail (v. 19).

Though it addresses a slightly different situation, Paul's teaching in 1 Corinthians 7 also seems relevant. Apparently, some individuals in that church thought their new life as a believer meant they had to change all the circumstances from their former life. Instead, Paul writes, they should remain in whatever state they were at the point of their salvation. He specifically mentions circumcision and slavery. The one who was circumcised prior to his conversion should not seek to "remove the marks of circumcision" or, conversely, now become circumcised (v. 18). The one who was a servant at the time of salvation should not be con cerned by that state, though if they can gain their freedom they should take advantage of that opportunity (v. 21).

This suggests that the Jewish ceremony of circumcision is unimportant. "For neither circumcision counts for anything nor uncircumcision" (v. 19). That same statement would seem to also apply to the matter of the Jewish ceremony of water baptism; neither its presence nor absence counts for anything. As long as it is not made a standard for judgment its practice is irrelevant. As those committed to the best possible alignment with scriptural teaching we prefer that water baptism not be any part of the church's practice. But if it's not made a standard of service it seems to be like circumcision as Paul discusses it in 1 Corinthians.

Still another variation is for a church to practice, even encourage, water baptism, to not require it for service, but make it a standard for membership. This is a logical position if baptism appears in the doctrinal statement, since doctrinal alignment is an appropriate expectation for membership. This, in turn, may exclude someone from certain positions within the church that require the individual to be a member. Certain leadership and teaching positions often require membership while other positions may not. In a case like this a mid-Acts dispensationalist will have to prayerfully consider all the factors involved including available church options and personal circumstances as mentioned above.

Should a mid-Acts dispensationalist submit to water baptism in order to fully enter into fellowship in a local church? Does doing so constitute an inappropriate compromise of one's conviction regarding scriptural teaching or only participation in what is an inconsequential ceremony (1 Cor. 7:19)?

In Romans 14 Paul writes that, "Each one should be fully convinced in his own mind (v. 5) and that "each of us will give an account of himself to God" (v. 12). Later in that chapter Paul writes, "But whoever has doubts is condemned if he eats, because the eating is not from faith. For whatever does not proceed from faith is sin" (v. 23). Thus, to submit to water baptism despite one's convictions to the contrary seems inappropriate and in violation of Paul's teaching in Romans 14. However, in this circumstance it may fall under the heading of inconsequential (1 Cor. 7:19). Each one of us answers to God (Rom. 14:10).

The practice of water baptism is the most common point of difference between a mid-Acts dispensationalists and the typical evangelical church including the dispensational church that begins the Body of Christ in Acts 2. If we assume that the practice of what are commonly (and incorrectly) called the charismatic gifts—speaking in tongues, prophecies, healings—is a barrier to fellowship (see Understanding Your Bible) then the next most likely issue relevant to fellowship is the matter of tithing. This seems like a surprising point of contention because Paul is so clear on the matter. But that tithing is found in the standards of some churches illustrates how common it is for tradition to influence a church's practice instead of Scripture.

Leviticus 27:30-33 makes it clear that the Israelites were to bring 10 percent of their income, regardless of its form, to the Lord. It belonged to God and could not be withheld without serious consequences. Tithing was not an option.

In Malachi 3:8-10 the prophet rebukes Israel for withholding the tithe, which amounts to robbing God. He tells them this sin has put the nation under a curse resulting in a famine that will only be lifted when they give to God what is his. If they do so God will "pour down for you a blessing until there is no more need" (v. 10). This passage demonstrates the importance of the tithe in God's relationship with Israel.

It's worth noting that the practice of the tithe predates the Mosaic law. In Genesis 14 we read the account of Abraham rescuing Lot from Chedorlaomer, King of Elam, who had defeated and plundered Sodom and Gomorrah including taking Lot and all his possessions. After returning from his rescue of Lot, Abraham was met by "Melchizedek, king of Salem," "priest of God Most High" (v. 18-20). Melchizedek, who most commentators agree is an Old Testament pre-incarnate appearance of Christ, blessed Abraham, who responded by giving Melchizedek "a tenth of everything" Abraham had taken in that battle.

In Genesis 28 we read the account of Jacob's dream of the ladder with angels ascending and descending. During that dream the Lord confirms to Jacob that he will fulfill the covenant made with Abraham and to Jacob his descendant. In the morning Jacob promises God that if he does indeed keep those promises "I will give a full tenth to you" (v. 22).

Both of these examples of the tithe occur hundreds of years before the tenth is made the standard in the Mosaic law. This suggests the tithe has some natural place in the order of spiritual things and that it came instinctively to these two patriarchs.

Paul makes it clear that a member of the Body of Christ should give whatever "he has decided in his heart, not reluctantly or under compulsion, for God loves a cheerful giver" (2 Cor. 9:7). This clearly contrasts with the requirement of the tithe in Leviticus 27 and serves as another example of the importance of the dispensational method. A church that makes the tithe a standard of fellowship has introduced a requirement inconsistent with God's teaching for the Body of Christ.

How do we reconcile what seems to be the natural base of the tithe as seen in Abraham and Jacob with Paul's statement that each one should give whatever they decide in their heart? A believer who has decided to give a proportion of their income to the Lord on a consistent basis ("as he may prosper" 1 Cor. 16:2) will often ask, "What is an appropriate amount of my income to give?" The biblical answer is, "Whatever you decide so long as it's at a level you can give cheerfully." But a place to begin when determining that proportion may be the tithe, the amount Abraham and Jacob instinctively gave to God. That may represent God's design. However, if one percent is the amount they feel is appropriate for them, no one can criticize that level as inadequate.

The tithe may be similar to the Sabbath. Both can be found in the biblical narrative prior to the Mosaic law as what seems to be God's

156

natural design for his people. That design is then formalized in the Mosaic law and made the required standard of behavior. In the dispensation of Grace those fixed requirements are set aside and no one can judge another based on them, but they still serve as a guide for the believer seeking to conform to God's design.

In an ideal world those who hold to a mid-Acts point for the beginning of the church, the Body of Christ would be able to attend a church that shares their view. However, that often isn't possible for a variety of reasons. This requires the believer to decide what constitutes a deviation that rules out a particular church as a place for worship, fellowship, and service. And that can vary depending on available options and the individual's life situation. As mentioned above, a parent has to consider the spiritual welfare of the children under their care when making a decision about what church to attend.

Paul's insistence on a gospel free from any trace of human works seems to rule out a church that teaches anything but faith in Christ's substitutionary atonement for salvation. Is water baptism, tithing, or some other action required for full participation in the life of the church? Here the answer may be more complicated. If circumcision or uncircumcision counts for nothing (1 Cor. 7:19) can the same be said about water baptism? Perhaps, but we also have to reckon with Paul's statement regarding the person who eats food he believes to be prohibited to the believer. "But whoever has doubts is condemned if he eats, because the eating is not from faith. For whatever does not proceed from faith is sin" (Rom. 14:23). Can the same be said about the believer who yields to a rite like water baptism that he understands to be contrary to biblical teaching for this dispensation but who goes through it to please others?

We may come to different conclusions on these difficult matters. Perhaps in this context the final word can also be found within the context of Paul's discussion of difficult matters. Earlier in Romans 14 Paul makes it clear that "Each one should be fully convinced in his own mind" (v.5), "For if we live, we live to the Lord, and if we die, we die to the Lord. So then, whether we live or whether we die, we are the Lord's" (v. 8). Believers should make these decisions carefully, seeking God's wisdom and guidance. The conclusions any individual Christian comes to are between them and the Lord and should not be subject to the judgment of others.

QUESTIONS

1. Why do you think support for the current state of Israel has become such an important issue among American evangelicals?
2. How would attention to Christ's teaching on prayer affect your practice of prayer?
3. Do you typically observe a Sabbath, a day of rest, in your life? How? And if not, how might you incorporate a regular break from your work? What would be the advantages of a Sabbath in your life?
4. If you don't attend a church that shares your dispensational perspective, what challenges does that present? If you do attend a church with a mid-Acts position, on what would you be willing to compromise if a move to another geographical area made that impossible.
5. We mentioned the Sabbath and tithing as practices that predate the Mosaic law and are made requirements for Israel. Can you think of any other practices that show up in the conduct of believers prior to the law that might serve as guidelines for us?

SOME CLOSING THOUGHTS

The evangelical church has gone through some dramatic changes in the last half century, affecting things like instruments used in worship, church architecture, and what people wear to a service. Many of these changes reflect developments taking place within general society as the church seeks to stay relevant. This is entirely appropriate where those changes don't affect biblical standards and the essentials of the faith. Scripture gives us no commands regarding the use of drums or the presence of a cross on the front wall. This hasn't stopped believers from engaging in bitter disputes over these and other equally unimportant matters, crippling the effectiveness of the church in the process.

Other developments have weakened the church and its ministries in the world. Large portions of evangelicalism have allowed shifts in societal values to alter their standards on topics like sexual purity and the nature of marriage.

A development more difficult to assess is the declining amount of focus on Christian doctrine and theology. It's probably fair to say that for too long churches drew strict lines over relatively minor doctrinal issues that became barriers preventing individual believers and congregations from fellowship and cooperation for the sake of the gospel. The emphasis on doctrinal differences also led to the impression among those outside of it that the church and the Bible are irrelevant to daily life. In some cases a concern for doctrinal purity kept churches from engaging with those around them, including those with physical and spiritual needs.

Conversely, the contemporary church largely ignores doctrine and theology in order to focus almost exclusively on issues of daily life. This results in a more relevant and engaged church but also has some very negative effects. For example, the vast majority of believers don't know the biblical words used to describe the salvation God has provided for them, can't identify the attributes of God, or are unable to communicate what the Bible teaches about
the deity of the incarnate Christ. To describe the typical contemporary believer as functionally illiterate regarding Christian doctrine isn't an overstatement.

The effects of this pendulum shift are potentially serious. It makes believers susceptible to false teaching with all its dangers. Paul wrote that one function of the leaders God has given to the church is "that we may no longer be children, tossed to and fro by the waves and carried about by every wind of doctrine, by human cunning, by craftiness in deceitful schemes" (Eph. 4:14). Too many Christians not grounded in biblical teaching have been drawn in by the prosperity gospel, by baseless promises of physical healing, and in some cases by false cults that claim to be Christian but pervert the gospel.

Christians who haven't yet learned the Bible's teaching on the nature of God cannot worship him with the appropriate measure of awe and reverence. Those who don't understand the sovereignty and goodness of God are susceptible to fear and despair when trials come. And those who don't know the nature of the gospel or the reality of eternal judgment cannot properly share with loved ones the good news of salvation.

Only a dispensational approach to the Bible, specifically one that understands Paul's role in the genesis of the Body of Christ, adequately answers the questions related to both doctrine and practice that face any believer who takes the Christian life seriously. Only Scripture makes us complete, equipped for every good work (2 Tim. 3:16), and only a mid-Acts dispensational approach correctly handles the Word (2 Tim. 2:15).

Balance in almost any area of life can be a challenge and requires we pay attention to and periodically assess the status of what may otherwise become competing dynamics with one aspect crowding out another. This leads us to ask what role theology and Dispensational theology in particular should have in the local church. How prominent should mid-Acts dispensationalism be in the teaching ministries of the church? How frequently should it be referenced in the pastor's sermon? As an interesting barometer of its emphasis, how long would a visitor attend before hearing about mid-Acts dispensationalism?

Certainly, there are no objective and fixed answers to those questions; they only help us assess the balance of Dispensational theology relative to the many other appropriate emphases in the ministries of the church.

In an effort to strike an appropriate balance regarding the place mid-Acts Dispensational theology should have in the local church it may help to reaffirm that its value is functional; that is, no benefit is derived from a thorough knowledge of the system unless it results in a more thorough knowledge of Scripture. Dispensationalism is a means to an end, specifically a better and more accurate understanding of God's Word. It is not an end in itself and therefore must not be the goal.

Understanding Dispensational theology is simply a means to an end—a better understanding of God's Word. The goal of understanding the Bible is to live its teachings. Paul said we are transformed by the renewing of our minds so that we can put God's will to the test and discover that it is good, pleasing, and perfect (Rom. 12:2). A knowledge of theology including Dispensational theology is, in itself, nothing commendable if it does not lead to a growing understanding of Scripture. That knowledge of Scripture, no matter how thorough, is meaningless if it does not lead to righteous living and a transformed life pleasing to our Savior.

Paul points out that "knowledge puffs up, but love builds up"

(1 Cor. 8:1). This plays out in the lives of too many mid-Acts dispensationalists who seem to have an attitude of superiority over brothers and sisters in Christ who don't have a similar grasp of mid-Acts dispensationalism. Like the Gnostics of the second century, these individuals have a pride problem wrapped in what they portray as a deeper commitment to the Bible.

Undertones of conflict between mid-Acts dispensationalists and other systems have historically characterized much of the literature written about Paul's unique ministry. This may trace back to a time generations ago when teachers and writers advocating for mid-Acts dispensationalism came under very harsh criticism from the leaders of denominations and other churches and responded in kind, or at least with defensiveness. In the current environment generally characterized by doctrinal and theological illiteracy, a combative spirit creates an unfavorable impression that becomes a barrier to the very goal these people profess—showing others the benefits of mid-Acts dispensationalism.

Another counterproductive behavior is referring to mid-Acts dispensationalists as "grace believers" or a particular congregation as a "grace church." As we saw in the section on Reformed theology all evangelicals share a commitment to salvation by grace including those who approach Scripture from the perspectives of Covenant theology. Attaching the adjective grace to a theological system or a particular congregation has the effect of implying others don't have an equal commitment to God's grace in either salvation or the Christian life. That would be both incorrect and ungracious.

We noted in *Understanding Your Bible* that the names traditionally given to the various dispensations are sometimes not the most helpful in terms of identifying the key feature of that dispensation. The dispensation of *Human Government* is probably the best example of a name that doesn't describe that dispensation's most prominent features, and that may leave a false impression, suggesting that human government didn't exist prior to this point in history.

This current dispensation of Grace received its name from Ephesians 3:2, "you have heard of the stewardship of God's grace that was given to me for you." The word here translated *stewardship* in the ESV is *oikonomia* in the Greek, translated dispensation in the KJV. This leads us to ask why Paul chose the word grace to describe the content of the mystery revealed to him by God.

Paul makes it very clear that salvation has always come through God's grace received by faith and never by human works (see Romans 4). Abraham was saved by God's grace as was everyone else before Paul's ministry. Why then does Paul describe this as the oikonomia of God's grace?

From God's choice of Abraham and his descendants in Genesis 12 until the beginning of this dispensation Gentiles were excluded from the promises and blessings of God (Eph. 2:11-12). The only way for a Gentile to approach God and receive salvation was through Israel, becoming what we now call a proselyte. With this dispensation, however, there is no distinction between Jews and Gentiles and we are now both reconciled to God by the cross, ending the hostility between us (Eph. 2:16).

Addressing his Gentile readers Paul writes, "So then you are no longer strangers and aliens, but you are fellow citizens with the saints and members of the household of God" (Eph. 2:19). In this context, just a few sentences later, Paul writes, "...assuming that you have heard of the stewardship of God's grace that was given to me for you" (Eph. 3:2). That is, God's salvation, now extended to Gentiles on an equal basis with the Jews, is such an outpouring of grace that Paul calls this the oikonomia of God's grace, not because it's present in a new way, but to a greater extent.

Failure to understand that Paul's stress is on the extent of God's grace has led some to conclude salvation involved works prior to this dispensation. That is a notion Paul rejected thoroughly. "For by the works of the law no human being will be justified in his sight, since through the law comes knowledge of sin" (Rom. 3:20).

Grace extended fully and equally to Gentiles led Paul to call this the oikonomia of grace, a name that certainly identifies the key feature of this dispensation. A case can be made that grace should also be the overriding character trait of members of the Body of Christ, who owe everything we are and will be to God's saving and sustaining grace. Those of us who hold a mid-Acts perspective should be known as particularly gracious.

Graciousness draws people to us, especially in an increasingly harsh and combative culture. Grace doesn't ignore truth or overlook differences, but it values people and sees them first and foremost as individuals loved by God and those for whom Christ died. Grace is gentle, never seeks revenge, and meets others' needs when possible. In short, being gracious is one characteristic of godliness.

Many contemporary believers have almost no understanding of basic theology, never mind the differences between Covenant and Dispensational theology. But they love and serve the Lord and his church and bear faithful witness to the gospel of salvation. Many who can give a thorough explanation of mid-Acts dispensationalism seem more concerned about accuracy in dispensational details than people.

If asked, would the apostle Paul or our heavenly Father say they'd prefer we have precise dispensational understanding of the Bible or a gracious heart for people and a burden for the gospel?

Thankfully, it is not an either/or situation. We can and should strive for both.

Made in the
USA
Middletown, DE